CIRCULAR WALKS
IN GOWER

Hazards and Problems
Take Notice, Take Care

The author and the publishers stress that walkers should be aware of the dangers that may occur on all walks.

- check local weather forecast before walking; do not walk up into mist or low clouds

- use local OS maps side by side with walking guides

- wear walking boots and clothing

- do not take any unnecessary risks – conditions can change suddenly and can vary from season to season

- take special care when accompanied by children or dogs

- when walking on roads, ensure that you are conspicuous to traffic from either direction

Circular Walks in Gower

Nick Jenkins

First edition: 1998
Revised edition: 2008
© Text: Nick Jenkins

ISBN: 978-1-84524-126-1

Cover design: Alan Jones

First published in 1998 by Gwasg Carreg Gwalch

Revised edition published in 2008 by Llygad Gwalch,
Ysgubor Plas, Llwyndyrys, Pwllheli, Gwynedd LL53 6NG
☎ 01758 750432   📠 01758 750438
📧 books@carreg-gwalch.com
Web site: www.carreg-gwalch.com

Circular Walks in Gower

If you thought you knew Gower, this is the book that might just prove you wrong! All parts of the peninsula are covered in 14 varied and circular walks. Not only is Gower's dramatic, and justly famous, cliff and coastal scenery explored but also the quieter, and equally attractive stretches of the less well known north coast. Add to this the quaint, rural charm of the inland farms and meadowlands and you have a guide that truly opens up one of Wales' most beautiful Areas of Outstanding Natural Beauty.

The book presents a lively potted history and geography of Gower to add interest to your walking adventures. Also included are some of the local lores and tales that add that magical ingredient that will really make you want to go out and see for yourself the place they call 'Little England Beyond Glamorgan'.

Each walk gives clear and concise directions, checked for accuracy by fellow walkers, and is accompanied by a sketch map. In addition, points of interest along the way are both highlighted and illustrated on the map.

Attractions in Gower include ancient tombs, medieval castles, nature reserves, and some of the best coastal scenery to be found anywhere. So come on, let's discover Gower together!

Contents

The Walks

Easy

Moderate

Strenuous

About the Author

Nick Jenkins is a keen walker and landscape photographer, having walked extensively both at home and abroad. His favourite areas are the Lake District, the Brecon Beacons, North Wales, the Yorkshire Dales, Pembrokeshire and now, Gower. He has also walked as far afield as the French Alps, Kashmir and Nepal, with his brother-in-law, Andrew Tomlin.

Nick has contributed a number of walks to walking magazines including 'High', and 'Country Walking'. A number of the walks in this book have previously appeared in 'Country Walking'.

Acknowledgements

The preparation of this book has taken up a considerable amount of my spare time over a period of some seven months. It has been a real labour of love even when trudging through the pouring rain, up to my fetlocks in mud, to meet deadlines. I thought I knew Gower but this project has shown me intimate corners of the peninsula that I never knew existed.

The production of the final manuscript has been greatly helped by the assistance and kindness of the locals who have stopped to chat and pass on useful titbits of information, which I, in turn, have been able to pass on to you. In particular, however, I would like to extend my gratitude to the following:

Steve Parry, Countryside Project Officer with the City and County of Swansea, for checking the walks for definitive rights of way; Mark Winder, Head Warden of the National Trust (Gower), for both supplying information relating to land owned and/or managed by the Trust, and providing some of the aforementioned titbits; D. M. Williams, the Recreation Officer of Forest Enterprise, for allowing access through the woods under their management; both Mike Hughes and David Pointer of the Countryside Council for Wales; Ordnance Survey for permission to base the sketch maps on the OS Explorer 10 map; Philippa and Barry Wood, for being 'guinea pigs', and testing out the walks for both interest and accuracy; and, finally, to my wife, Anne and my son, Stephen, for putting up with my absences (sometimes more happily than I'm prepared to admit).

LOCATION MAP

- Whiteford Sands
- Broughton Bay
- Llanmadoc •
- **9**
- **6**
- Rhossili Bay
- **12**
- Worms Head
- Rhossili • Middleton •
- **4**
- Llangenydd •
- **7** Reynoldston •
- **5**
- **14**
- Oxwich •
- **8**
- Porteynon • Horton •
- **13**
- **2**
- Cheriton •
- **1**
- **10**
- Llanrhidian •
- Penmaen •
- **3**
- Southgate •
- **11**
- Swansea Bay
- Mumbles Head

Introduction

Maybe I should confess right up front that I am not a 'Gowerian'. I have links with Gower, albeit somewhat tenuous (I spent many happy childhood summers at Oxwich and have an uncle who lives on the outskirts of Swansea) but I was not born there and I have never lived there. Nevertheless, I have an abiding love of this beautiful peninsula and have passed very many happy hours walking its footpaths and wandering somewhat aimlessly along its breathtaking clifftops.

I have jotted down, therefore, a few introductory notes; a backdrop almost, to Gower, or to Welsh speakers, Gwyr, (not *The* Gower, unless you want to incur the wrath of the locals) as an attempt to give a feel for the area in terms of its history and landscape. These are in no way meant to be exhaustive but merely to serve as a flavour, or hors d'oeuvre for what is to come as your walks lead you to explore and enquire. If you have an appetite to learn more the selected bibliography at the back will hopefully help point you in your chosen direction. Two books in particular will, however, provide you with a very good grounding of Gower. These are *The Story of Gower* by Wendy Hughes, published by Gwasg Carreg Gwalch, and *A Guide to Gower* published by The Gower Society.

Gower was the first area in Britain to be designated as an Area of Outstanding Natural Beauty (AONB) in 1956. What makes it so especially rich for those who enjoy exploring on foot is not only the scenery, ranging as it does from gentle to dramatic, but also the feeling that you are almost in a country apart from the rest of South Wales. Geographically this feeling is well supported by the somewhat remote and almost island-like nature of the peninsula. But there seems more to it than just hard geography. There are the people, the place names, the ancient cromlechs, the castles, and above all, that certain indefinable something that here is somewhere special. And unless you get out of your car and walk you will undoubtedly miss out on all that this mini-paradise has to offer.

A cursory glimpse of the maps of Gower will indicate an almost Welsh/English divide of the peninsula. The area to the north of Cefn Bryn (traditionally north of Arthur's Stone, on the west end of the ridge) is predominantly Welsh and the area to the south mostly English. In fact, a certain Mr. Edward Lhuyd, keeper of the Ashmolean Museum at Oxford in the late 17th century, referred to the inhabitants of South Gower as Gower Anglicana, and to those from the north as Gower Wallicana. In the north are the villages of Llanrhidian, Llanmorlais, Llanmadog and Penclawdd, whereas in the south are to be found Oxwich, Port Eynon, Parkmill and Reynoldston.

All too often, the enduring memory of a day out in Gower is of being stuck in a traffic jam; cars in front of you, cars behind you, tall hedges either side of you and the odd glimpse of a sandy bay away in the distance before it is time to turn round and head for home. Yet, it really need not be so. The whole of the peninsula of Gower, measuring just 19 miles long by between 3 and 8 miles wide, is a treasure house for those who love good country walking. Here you will discover a wonderful microcosm of all that the Welsh landscape can throw at you; almost a country in miniature. There is windswept moorland in the shape of Cefn Bryn and Rhossili Downs; wild and dramatic clifftop walking along the southern coastline; broad sandy beaches at Oxwich, Rhossili and Whiteford; expansive salt marshes off Llanrhidian and quiet leafy lanes practically everywhere. The grades of walking vary from easy to quite strenuous, although grading is dictated more by the length of the walk than by the severity of the terrain covered, nowhere on Gower being particularly testing for the reasonably fit. More of this later.

The main objective of this guide, therefore, is to share with you, the discerning walker, the explorations and discoveries that I have enjoyed of the 'inner sanctum' that really represents Gower, its people and its ways.

Brief History

Perhaps the best place to start our walk through Gower's history is at the last ice-age, when the Bristol Channel was a wide river valley, with the tall limestone cliffs of South Gower facing towards it. The valley would have supported enough animal and plant life to sustain those hunter gatherers who occupied caves in the cliffs, such as Paviland, Minchin Hole, Bacon Hole, and Leathers Hole. These have all revealed evidence of human occupation as well as remains of animals such as mammoth, hyena, wolf and soft nosed rhinoceros.

Slowly, agriculture replaced hunting as the main means of supporting human life and with it came farmers and the communities that sprang up around them. Around 4000BC came the introduction of communal tombs or burial chambers, erected by Neolithic, or New Stone Age Man. There are some fine examples of these, the best being found at Parkmill (Parc le Breos burial chamber, known locally as the Giant's Grave), Penmaen (Pen y Crug), Cefn Bryn (Arthur's Stone) and Rhossili Down (Sweyne's Houses). The remarkable Neolithic chambered tomb of Arthur's Stone is shrouded in mystery and is thought by some to be the Maen Ceti, one of the wonders of the ancient Isle of Britain. The tomb seems to have earned its name from the legend that the capstone was once a pebble which found its way into King Arthur's shoe on his way to a battle hereabouts. Having extracted the offending piece of rock he flung it as far as he could and it landed at Cefn Bryn, an Olympian throw of some 7 miles from where King Arthur stood. Whatever the history and origin of the stone there can surely be no doubting the tale that each New Year's Eve (or Midsummer's Eve, according to some) the stone walks down to the sea at Burry Pill for a drink of water.

The next significant milestone in Gower's history is represented by the Iron Age. Iron-using warriors crossed the English Channel, having migrated up from Iberia, and started to populate Britain around 500BC. They built up strong fortifications to defend their newly acquired lands. Perhaps the best example of this is to be found at Cil Ifor Top, built on a rounded hill of millstone grit, near Llanrhidian. The fort covers around 8 acres, and was protected by 3 large ramparts. Another Iron Age fort is to be found nearby, at The Bulwark, on the eastern side of Llanmadog Hill. The construction and plan of both forts is quite complex and suggests that they were developed and enlarged over a fair number of years. The inhabitants of a third hillfort, on Harding's Down, were reputedly involved in a right old bust up with the warriors of The Bulwark, the blood running so deep from the carnage as to form a lake nearby, known today as Tankeylake, or Tonkin's Lake, Tonkin being the leader from The Bulwark, who was slain in the battle.

The Vikings, or Norsemen, were to next to come knocking. They are not believed to have really settled in the peninsula but certainly some of Gower's place names, such as Worm's Head and Burry Holms, live on.

The Norman invasion is the next landmark in Gower's history. Not long after 1066 Gower was annexed as a Norman Lordship, and given to Henry de Newburgh, the first Lord of Gower. Prior to this it had been the Welsh cantref of Gwyr, and before this again part of the ancient kingdom of Deheubarth. Swansea was the 'capital' with a large castle being built at Oystermouth. Whilst it is true that there were the odd rebellious skirmishes they were of limited impact and little success over the stranglehold imposed by the Norman Lords and their English followers. Gower belonged to the Normans. Interestingly, one of the consequences of the Norman presence was the opening up of Gower to folk from the West Country, mainly from Devon and Somerset. This was a major factor in the anglicising of South Gower as noted earlier, demonstrated by the place names and the way of life. North Gower retained its Welshness to a greater extent, being more exposed to the uplands and valleys occupied by the indigenous Welsh peoples.

Subsequent Gower history was greatly influenced by the presence of two families, whose activities were as much a part of Gower as Gower was a part of them. Perhaps the most influential were the Mansel family. They originally inhabited Penrice Castle, moving on to Oxwich Castle and then on to Margam, near Port Talbot. They were associated with high office (Sir John Mansel was Lord Chancellor to King Henry III) as well as low office, in the form of smuggling, shipwrecking and other 'ne'er do well' activities. It was a member of the Mansel family, Sir Edward Mansel, who is alleged to have made off with the lion's share of treasure taken from a wrecked Portuguese galleon off the Rhossili coast at the end of the 17th century. He disappeared on the night of the shipwreck, supposedly murdered for his newly acquired booty. Another school of thought puts this timely disappearance to Sir Edward putting as much distance as possible between himself and those who would relieve him of his gold. Either way, it is said that his ghostly carriage still races across Rhossili sands pulled by four grey horses. In the 18th century the Rev. Thomas Talbot of Laycock Abbey, in Wiltshire, married Mary Mansel, the Mansel fortunes being absorbed into the newly formed Mansel Talbot family. The name of the Mansel family lives on, however, in place names such as Manselton, Manselfield, Manselfold and the standing stone of Mansel Jack, near Manselfold Farm. Incidentally, the medieval looking castle walls near Penrice Castle on the junction of the road leading down to Oxwich are in fact a sham, or folly. They were built in 1780 by one Anthony Kelk for the occupant of Penrice, Thomas Talbot.

Another well known Gower family were the Lucases. Although originally from Shenfield, in Essex, they were well established in the peninsula by the end of the Middle Ages. Their most enduring monument is the mansion of Stouthall (originally a smaller dwelling known as Stoutwalls) on the main Port Eynon road, just before the village of Knelston. It is now an outdoor education centre for the London Borough of Merton. One of their most visible and interesting legacies, however, is the ruin of Salthouse Mansion, found on the west side of Port Eynon beach, and supposedly built to support the process of extracting salt from sea water. Another story tells us it earned its name because the outer walls were washed by salt sea water owing to its proximity to the tide-line. It was built, or at least made more habitable, by David Lucas in the 16th century for his son John Lucas. The ruins seen today are the remains of old fishermen's cottages, built on the site of the former manor.

Linked to Salthouse, and not too far away to the west, is the mysterious Culver Hole; a gash in the cliff nearby, walled up, but with windows built in, and a stairway inside. It has been variously described as a columbarium (a source of fresh pigeon meat), an arms stronghold and/or a smugglers' retreat for John Lucas, who seemed to fluctuate between being a pirate, a smuggler and a local Robin Hood. The truth is that no-one really knows for certain when it was constructed or why (although its antiquity is in little doubt) but evidence seems to indicate that it served all three purposes at some time or another. Fairly easy to get to, it never fails to surprise those who suddenly come across it built into the cliff.

Gower has a rich history of smuggling. All levels of society seemed to have an involvement as we have just seen. With so much rugged coastline and so many hidden bays and coves this probably comes as no surprise. This nefarious activity would have been reinforced by the high levels of taxes then imposed on luxury goods such as alcohol, tobacco and fine laces, and the popularity of the Bristol Channel as a busy shipping route. Pretty well all of the coastal (and not so coastal) villages had a hand in these grisly goings-on. After all, how do you think Brandy Cove earned its name? (It is a bit more swash-buckling than Hareslade Bay, the original name for it.)

Tales exist, too, of the locals deliberately wrecking ships along the rocky coastline for plunder. It is quite probable that some of these are however, just that - tales, made up about a hundred years ago to entertain and should be treated with appropriate caution. According to these stories a favourite spot for luring these poor victims to their fate was the isthmus between Worms Head and the Rhossili headland, known locally as The Causeway. We are told of young boys and girls being made to walk back and fore along the clifftops waving lanterns to give the impression to ships' crews of safe harbour nearby, only to have their hopes, and their cargo laden vessels dashed as they were cruelly tricked onto the rocks. The ships' crews would all be murdered to prevent these foul deeds from being brought to the attention of the wrong people. Whilst this was all pretty ghoulish, and perhaps somewhat fanciful, it does add rather a touch of derring-do to the folklore of the area, and makes it none the less interesting for that. It is almost certainly true to say, however, that should a ship be unfortunate enough to be dashed against the rocks (and many were) the cargo would mysteriously disappear in very little time at all.

The Landscape

It is the variety of landscapes that really give Gower its appeal. These in turn are directly attributable to the geology of the peninsula. The nature of the rock dictates the nature of the soil and this in turn dictates the nature of the flora and fauna that best survive on it.

As noted previously, Gower ranges from moorland terrain through deep wooded valleys to rocky cliffs and sandy beaches. Thrown in for good measure is a wide expanse of salt marsh. Intertwined with, and integral to this diverse landscape is the evidence of man's handiwork, in the form of ancient cromlechs, standing stones and castles.

The majority of Gower lies on rather blocky carboniferous limestone, laid down about 280 million years ago. It is this limestone which gives us the majestic succession of cliffs, from Mumbles right along the coast to Worms Head, with a defiant upthrust at Broughton (pronounced 'Bruffton') Bay. The depth of the limestone belt here is the deepest in South Wales, being just under 4000 feet (1220 metres) thick at Port Eynon. Most of this, of course, is below ground, the highest clifftop point in Gower being Pwlldu Head, rising to 320 feet (97 metres).

A footpath follows this cliff line, offering stunning views of the rocks and crags rising and folding sheer out of the sea. They are only broken to cross or skirt sandy beaches, narrow coves and sand dunes. Here is a real paradise for both botanists and ornithologists alike. A variety of colourful flowers exist along this stretch, seen at its best in May and June, including orchids, evening primrose, birdsfoot trefoil ('bacon and eggs' to my Mum and Dad), cranesbill and everywhere the sight and heady scent of the ubiquitous yellow gorse bush. Over 100 species of plants have been recorded in the sand dunes of Nicholaston Burrows alone, many of them extremely rare. This is ably abetted by the splashes of lichen; green and yellow, liberally dotted over the rocks, like an artist's palette. For the birdwatchers, Worms Head can offer guillemots, kittiwakes and razorbills. Elsewhere, look out for cormorants and shags drying their wings on the offshore rocks, or on the railings around the old iron lighthouse off Whiteford Burrows. Although cormorants confine their breeding to the south coastline, they are frequently seen around here, at the mouth of the Burry estuary. I have on occasions seen choughs in South Gower too; an uncommon (in Britain) member of the crow family, noted for its red beak and legs, and its noisy, high pitched call as it echoes around the cliffs.

The higher reaches of the peninsula, Cefn Bryn, Rhossili Down and Llanmadog Hill, are all formed from Devonian, or old red sandstone, revealed where the limestone has been subjected to weathering and has eroded away, revealing the older layer underneath. The sandstone is much older than the limestone, being laid down some 350 million years ago. This rock, an unyielding conglomerate containing quartzite, has resisted nature's attempts to weather it down. It stands proud, overseeing the plateau spread out below it. Indeed, from the Cefn Bryn ridge, the whole of Gower is laid out at your feet. The terrain here comprises heather and tussocky grass more reminiscent of upper moorland country. Along the length of the ridge runs a track, from Arthur's Stone to Penmaen, a lofty route with excellent views all round.

The Llanrhidian marshes should not go unsung. Whilst they may lack the punch of cliff scenery there is still an abundance of wildlife here too. Look out especially for marsh harriers, kestrels and, if you're very lucky, peregrine falcons. Orchids flower in profusion on Whiteford Burrows in June as though their very lives depended it.

The Walks

As mentioned earlier, it is really the nature of the terrain which prevents walks in Gower being graded in terms of severity. Nowhere is the walking difficult (unless you are singularly unfit or overweight). The greatest challenges to your legs will probably be the ascents and descents along the cliff path of South Gower, but it has to be said that even these are not particularly arduous. Probably the longest sustained stretch of uphill walking is the ascent of Rhossili Down, either from the north or the south end. And basically, that's it. Walking in Gower is always a pleasure, never a pain. For this reason I have graded the walks more in terms of their length than their severity. Entirely arbitrarily I have elected to grade the walks based on the following criteria:

- up to 3 miles (4.8 kilometres)   Easy   (Short)
- from 3 to 5 miles (4.8 to 8 kilometres)   Moderate   (Medium)
- over 5 miles (8 kilometres)   Strenuous   (Long)

The introduction to each walk does, however, indicate the nature of the terrain that you will encounter, and I have not allowed myself to become hidebound by the above yardsticks if it doesn't seem sensible to do so.

All distances are quoted in good old imperial measurements but have their metric equivalent bracketed after them - on occasions this does look a little clumsy, ('about 92 metres' somehow doesn't convey the same meaning as 'about 100 yards') but nevertheless both are there to act as a guide. Neither measurement should be construed as being absolutely definitive.

The walks have been presented in these groupings to make it easier to select the walk you want to do that day when compared with other walks in that group. This might depend on such factors as the weather, your level of fitness or simply the mood you are in. Generally allow about 1 hour for every 2 miles (3.2 kilometres). This is fairly leisurely and allows for whizzing downhill and slogging up the other side. On this basis a 5 mile (8 kilometres) walk should take about 2½ hours. This will, of course, vary from one pair of legs to another (and, should it come on to rain, you may decide to run the last stretch anyway). This is offered as a guide and should not be slavishly adhered to. But then you are walkers, aren't you, otherwise you wouldn't have bought this book. So you already know all this. Similarly, you will know to expect the bit you find in all walking guides about wearing sensible footwear. I know you have read it before, but you would probably not believe what I have seen the more fashion conscious struggling with down a loose and scrabbly cliff path. In line with the supplication on sturdy and appropriate footwear comes the need to dress sensibly and appropriately. This needn't involve being kitted up for a Himalayan hike (unless that is your inclination) but should include waterproofs and a spare pullover. Take a fairly small but comfortable day sack with you. For the walks in this book anything over about 25 litres capacity can become burdensome.

All the walks in this guide are covered by the Ordnance Survey's maps, Landranger Number 159, covering Swansea, Gower and the Surrounding Area, and Explorer Number 10, confined to Gower. Each walk in the book is accompanied by a sketch map but this is really only meant as a guide, and should be treated thus. The map should be your bible. The sketch maps do, however, show the points of interest detailed after each walk, the number of each point corresponding with the text.

It is also important to note that whilst every effort has been made to ensure that the details contained in the walks are as up to date as possible, nothing stands still, not least the rural countryside. From time to time, gates appear or disappear; stiles are renewed or upgraded; paths are renewed, extended, diverted or even closed altogether. On more than one occasion whilst compiling this guide I have had to revise walk details where a gate suddenly decided to become a stile, or a green lane had been blocked off! Hopefully, such changes in detail should be fairly minor, (I will have picked up on any major changes) and not detract from the enjoyment of the walk. Any difficult or dangerous obstructions, however, should be reported to the team at the 'Rights of Way' Office at the City and County of Swansea Council.

The City and County of Swansea is the highway authority responsible for public rights of way i.e. footpaths, bridleways and byways within its area.

The 'Rights of Way' team is based in the Countryside and Nature Conservation Section of the Planning Department. In brief the work of the team involves the following:

1. Maintaining and keeping under review the definitive map - this is the legal document relating to rights of way.

2. The team has a duty to sign all rights of way where they meet a metalled road and has a power to install signs and directional waymarks to assist landowners with rights of way on their property and to ensure people using them are on the correct line.

3. Network maintenance - the team is active in maintaining and, where possible, improving rights of way within the Authority's area.

4. Legal matters - the Authority has legal powers to enforce and protect the public's right to use and enjoy rights of way and also to undertake diversions and modification orders where deemed necessary by law.

There are 600 kilometres of rights of way within the City and County of Swansea. The 'Rights of Way' team relies heavily on reports from walkers, riders and other users on conditions, obstructions or general problems encountered. Should you have anything to report, as mentioned earlier, or want further information about these routes or the wider network then please contact:

The Rights of Way Officer
Planning Department
City and County of Swansea
The Guildhall
SWANSEA
SA1 4PH
Tel: (01792) 635230
Fax: (01792) 635709
e-mail: sccplan@dircom.co.uk

Welsh Place-names

By and large the majority of Welsh place-names appear in the north of Gower, although some do pop up in the south as well. Below are some of the more common Welsh words to be found in Gower place-names. I have ordered them as they are found in the village or place-names rather than alphabetically. It can be fun getting to grips with what the Welsh name means and clues can be revealed as to how or why that name came to be.

Pen – *head or top*
Rhos – *moorland*
Llan – *church, or holy place*
Cefn – *ridge*
Bryn – *hill*
Cwm – *valley*
Cil – *in the shadow of*
Mynydd – *hill or mountain*
Hen – *old*
Llys – *court*

Maen – *rock or stone*
Pwll – *pool*
Du – *black*
Gwern – *alder grove*
Ffrwd – *stream*

Do not make the mistake of trying to locate the village of Llwybr Cyhoeddus, liberally signposted but never found. It is Welsh for public footpath (just look on the other side of the sign if you do not believe me).

Conservation

One last but vitally important point bears emphasising before we set off on our walks. Gower is a relatively small area with increasing pressure to provide leisure and amenity to an ever growing tourist influx. The recent improvements in the road network, especially recent additions and improvements to the M4 motorway bring Gower so much closer to not only the population of South East Wales but also to the South and West of England. There are certain things that we walkers, as a constituent part of this tourist demand, can do to help preserve Gower for both our own and our children's enjoyment. Always walk with care and consideration; marching up a hill, ten abreast will do wonders for erosion and the resulting scars will take much longer to heal than they do to create! Be aware of, and considerate towards, your environment. Gower is rightly proud of several species of flora exclusive to this area. Don't pick them! Similarly, don't jettison your rubbish en route. There are few sights more ugly (and environmentally damaging) than discarded drink cans, bottles and crisp wrappers. They were in your rucksack when full so they can't be that much of a burden to carry back when they're empty! Remember, above all, that Gower is there to be enjoyed - but not just by you.

The Country Code

- enjoy the countryside and respect its life and work
- guard against all risk of fire
- keep your dog under control
- keep to public paths across farmland
- use gates and stiles to cross fences, hedges and walls
- leave livestock, crops and machinery alone
- take your litter home
- help to keep all water clean
- protect wildlife, plants and trees
- take special care on country roads
- don't make any unnecessary noise

As the old adage eloquently puts it, 'leave nothing but footprints, take nothing but memories' (or photographs, depending on where you may have previously read it!).

Along the Marsh's Edge
(Llanrhidian - Weobley Castle - Llanrhidian)

Access:	The walk starts and ends in the village of Llanrhidian. Leave Swansea through Gowerton and pass through Penclawdd to Llanrhidian. Alternatively, leave Swansea through Upper Killay, cross Fairwood Common on the road signposted to Llanrhidian. Turn right off the main road down to the village .
Start/Parking:	Park (thoughtfully) in Llanrhidian. Grid ref. 497923
Distance/Grade:	About 3 miles (4.8 km) - Easy; a pleasant stroll through typical North Gower countryside. Doing the walk in the direction described offers up the most dramatic views of Weobley Castle.
Terrain:	The walk covers footpaths across fields, farm tracks and country lanes. There are a number of stiles, none of which have dog passes. The tracks can be muddy, so come prepared from the knees down.
Facilities:	The Welcome to Town Inn is situated near the start. However, it has recently changed hands and was closed during my last visit. Check carefully before setting off. There are loos at Weobley Castle, along with a small souvenir shop.

The Walk:

With the church on your right and the Welcome to Town Inn on your left, walk uphill for about 20 yards (18 metres) as far as the telephone box near Cross House. Turn right past the telephone box and continue

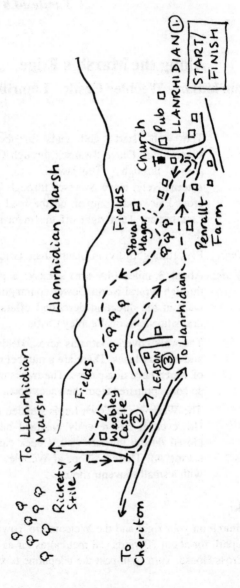

Along The Marsh's Edge

along the lane. Just past a barn on your left turn right along a path, passing a garage on your right. Continue ahead, keeping the wall of the church on your right. After about 100 yards (91 metres), join a clear track, and turn left, signposted 'Weobley Castle 2km'.

Keep with the track as it skirts the base of the wooded hillside up on your left. Ignore a driveway leading down to Staval Hagar but continue ahead along the track. The route ahead is fairly obvious as it crosses a number of stiles, keeping the fields to your right and the wooded slopes to your left. At the end of the second field past Staval Hagar, ignore a signposted path leading off left to Leason Woods but again continue ahead, along the path, hugging the upper edge of the fields.

Four fields past the path to Leason Woods the path turns into a rough stony track, heading left and uphill. Follow the track for about 50 yards (46 metres), and look carefully for a stile on your right. Cross the stile to cross some rough scrubland and emerge over another stile into a field. About ½ way between this stile and Weobley Castle, rising up on your left, turn left over a stile and out of the field. Follow the path as it turns immediately right to contour the hill through some more scrub. Leave the path over another stile, almost immediately below the castle to pick up a clear farm track.

Turn left along the track and, where it bends sharp left and starts to ascend cross a wooden stile on your right. Take care here; the stile is rather rickety, but is due to be replaced in the near future. At this point the footpath should follow over a stile on the right after about 75 yards (68 metres). This is currently impassable, the surrounding area being used for field archery. Instead, turn left and keep to the sheep track running dead ahead up the hill through the field and midway between the hillsides. Near the top of the hill turn left and cross a stile, beside a gate, onto the lane leading back to Weobley Castle. (There is a concrete lane to the left of the field path that appears to offer a shortcut - a continuation of the track joined just past the castle. It is, however, private farmland, containing a control gate for the sheep. Careless walkers have ascended by this track in the past and left the gate at the top open - the owner, Mr Pritchard, does not find it funny when sheep wander through down to the marshes at high tide).

This is the point from which to visit the castle should you so wish. A charge is payable at the small shop attached to the nearby farm. From here, turn right to join the lane leading on to Llanmadoc. Turn left into the lane, and, after about 200 yards (182 metres), turn left over a stone stile into a field. Turn right and cross the corner of the field to another stile. Continue along the indistinct path, connected by very distinct stiles (and one wooden swing gate), to cross a further three fields. At the end of the third field cross two stiles to enter a rough lane. Continue along the lane passing a large farm garden on your left. Where this track joins the track leading down to the farm, turn right to continue to the small hamlet of Leason.

Pass through Leason, ignoring the access lane coming in from the right. Instead, continue ahead to a solitary house (the last house in Leason). Cross a stile to the right of the house, and turn left along the fenced edge of a field. Look for a stile to your right and cross this into another field. Continue ahead along the left edge of the field, and cross a stile in its top left hand corner. Pass into another field and make for the stile ahead. Cross the stile to enter a rather muddy 'cow run'. Continue ahead along the path, following the yellow waymark arrows to pass through a farmyard and then past a farmhouse on your left. Pass through an iron gate, and stay with the path as it becomes a little indistinct, but always waymarked. By now, Llanrhidian church tower is clearly visible down on your left.

At the remains of an old quarry, covered in vegetation, turn right, again guided by the waymark arrow, and stay with the path as it leads to a lane of houses at the top of Llanrhidian. Pass between the houses, and 20 yards (18 metres) later, turn left, downhill. Continue down the lane to join the point at which you earlier turned right at the start of the walk. From here continue along the lane, past the barn, now on your right, and pass Cross House on your left to emerge back in the middle of Llanrhidian near the church and the start of the walk.

Points of Interest:

1. Llanrhidian is a small village described by local guide books as being estuarine. The village gets its name from the church of St Rhidian (also dedicated to St Illtyd). The church is well worth

exploring. Whilst there look out for 'The Leper Stone', dug up outside the church porch some time during the last century. How it came to be where it was found is a mystery but its antiquity is in little doubt; the animal engravings appear to resemble bears and the stone is believed to have originated with the Norsemen. Apparently, it is the only stone of its kind in Wales.

The village was once a centre for sheep rearing, the nearby cottage of Staffal Haegr (or Staval Hagar) once being a woollen mill producing a cloth called 'minka'. This was a coarse striped cloth once frequently worn by miners, quarrymen and tin-plate workers throughout South Wales.

2. The spectacularly positioned Weobley Castle is more of a fortified manor than a true castle. It is believed to have been built in the 13th century by the Norman De la Bere family who lived there for some 200 years. The castle was badly mauled in 1409 by the soldiers of Owain Glyndwr, Sir John De la Bere being its less than happy incumbent. Subsequent owners have included Sir Rhys ap Thomas, who made good Glyndwr's handiwork and even extended the castle further. Later owners included the Herberts and the Mansels. In 1911, Miss Mansel Talbot, of Penrice, handed it over to the Ministry of Works. Today it is in the capable hands of Cadw and is open to the public. Botanists have a certain interest in Weobley Castle, its high walls playing host to some 30 different species of flowering plants, including wallflowers and a variety of ferns.

3. Leason is a small hamlet, previously associated with the weaving trade. Of greater interest is the local legend of the 'Scanderoon'. It is said that hundreds of years ago the 'Scanderoon' became stranded on the mudflats hereabouts, spilling its cargo of gold bullion chests. All the chests except one were recovered. Some years later a local man suddenly, and unaccountably, came into a fortune. Was there a connection? If so, apparently nothing was ever proved - another one of Gower's many mysteries.

Sneaking Up on Ryers Down

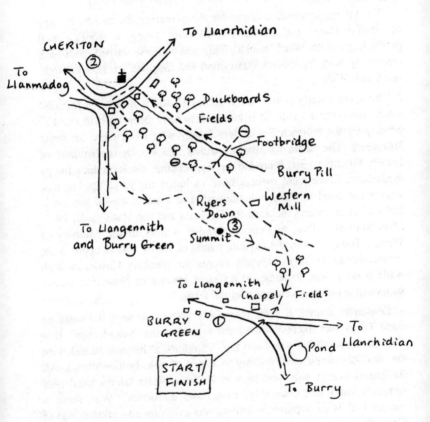

CHERITON

To Llanmadog

To Llanrhidian

②

Duckboards

Fields

Footbridge

Burry Pill

Western Mill

Ryers Down

To Llangennith
and Burry Green

Summit ③

To Llangennith

Chapel

Fields

BURRY GREEN ①

To Llanrhidian

Pond

START/FINISH

To Burry

Sneaking up on Ryer's Down
(Burry Green - Cheriton - Burry Green)

Access: The walk starts and ends in the village of Burry Green. Leave Swansea by the B4271 across Fairwood Common. Pass Llanrhidian and where the road splits at Oldwalls, take the left fork to Burry Green.

Start/Parking: Park in Burry Green. Grid ref. 463914.

Distance/Grade: About 3 miles (4.8 km). Easy; a beautiful country stroll. Especially rewarding on a fine autumn day.

Terrain: The walk covers fields, farm tracks, woodland and moorland.

Facilities: None on route.

The Walk:

From Bethesda Chapel, walk back along the main road in the direction of Swansea for about 100 yards (91 metres). Turn left through a waymarked gate, and walk up the left hand side of a field. Pass through a gate into a second field. Keeping the hedge on the left make for the top left hand corner. Cross a stile into a plantation of young trees, to leave it over another stile. Cross a path at right angles and continue ahead, downhill, to a track.

Turn left along the track to pass the small farm of Western Mill on the right. The track becomes a path at this point and continues ahead to enter woodland. Take the track leading to the right and downhill, to cross the Burry Stream, or Pill, over an old stone bridge. Cross a stile on the left to enter a field. Continue ahead along the bottom edge of the field, keeping the Burry Stream on your left. Cross four stiles before entering woodland. The path through the woods is a bit vague (helped in parts by the presence of duckboarding) but continue dead ahead (avoiding obviously large trees) to emerge in a field over another stile. Continue ahead along the edge of the field to a metal stile. Cross the stile into the main road through Cheriton, opposite the church of St Cadoc, or Cattwg.

Turn left down the road and, where it bends sharply to the right, take the second (higher) of two tracks off to the left. The correct track has a sign for Hillside, a house passed on the right. The track becomes a green lane as it enters woodlands. Continue to ascend the hill through the woods to emerge on the road connecting Llangennydd with Llanmadoc. Turn left along the road and after about 400 yards (366 metres) turn left over a waymarked stile, and continue ahead, keeping the hedge in front on your left. Cross the next stile and keep ahead for a short distance, to cross another stile to your right. Incline slightly right to meet a cinder track.

Turn left along the track, in the direction of Ryer's Down. After about 100 yards (91 metres), take an obvious path leading off at a 45 degree angle to the right, and follow this as it directly ascends the Down to the trig point. From the trig point there are extensive views in all directions, but the view to the north over Llanrhidian Marshes is outstanding. Continue ahead along the same obvious path to descend the eastern flank of the Down. About half way down the descent climb over the stile on your right, crossed earlier in the walk. Re-enter the plantation, to emerge from it over the second stile.

From here simply retrace your steps across the two fields to the main road and turn right back to Burry Green.

Points of Interest:

1. Burry Green really lives up to its name, there being a wide Green here, playing host to two ponds with all their resident wildlife. The first Methodist chapel in Gower was built here, in 1814, at the behest of Lady Barham, of nearby Fairy Hill. She rather saw herself as the evangelical saviour of the sinners around her and followed up with a

string of other chapels. She was, by all accounts, endowed with incredible energy and single-mindedness. It is said that if she disapproved of a sermon, she would signal it by simply walking out of the chapel. One did not cross Lady Barham without giving considerable thought to the consequences.

2. Cheriton is more of a large hamlet than a small village but nonetheless proudly boasts the most beautiful church in Gower. Dedicated to St. Cadoc, or Cattwg, it was, in common with most Gower churches, built in the 13th century. In 1770, the peaceful churchyard was said to have been the scene of a brawl over land rights, between two factions of the ubiquitous Lucas family. The story goes that the Rector was locked in the church, 'it being offensive to shed blood in sight of clergy'. The nearby Glebe Farm is believed to date from the 15th century and was probably once a hostel built by the Knights Hospitallers of St. John of Jerusalem, whose local headquarters were in Slebech, in Pembrokeshire.

3. The hill of Ryer's Down consists of hard, resistant old red sandstone, poking up through the surrounding layer of limestone. This hard rock was the source of many of Gower's millstones, and is also found on Rhossili Down and Cefn Bryn.

Step Into Tranquility

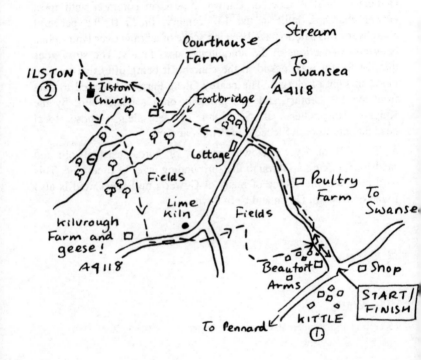

Stream

Courthouse Farm

ILSTON ②

Ilston Church

Footbridge

To Swansea
A4118

Cottage

Fields

Poultry Farm

To Swansea

Lime Kiln

Fields

kilvrough Farm and geese!

A4118

Beaufort Arms

□ Shop

START/ FINISH

To Pennard

KITTLE ①

Step into Tranquility
(Kittle - Ilston - Kittle)

Access:	The walk starts and ends in the village of Kittle. Leave Swansea through Bishopston, to Kittle.
Start/Parking:	At Kittle Green, near the Beaufort Arms. Grid ref. 574893.
Distance/Grade:	About 3 miles(4.8 km). Easy; a pleasant stroll in the country.
Terrain:	The walk covers country lanes, farm tracks, green lanes and paths across fields and through woodland
Facilities:	The Beaufort Arms in Kittle (either at the start or the end!). There is a grocery shop across the road from the Beaufort Arms, and a Post Office and General Store almost next door but nothing else on the route (unless you opt for the 'there and back' detour down Ilston Cwm to the Gower Inn at Parkmill - see walk details).

The Walk:

Keeping the Beaufort Arms on your left walk along Kittle Hill Lane, passing bungalows on both sides of the lane. At the point where the lane clearly narrows to a single track width, cross the stile on the right and walk along the left hand edge of the field, parallel to the lane. At the large poultry farm (Stonegate Farmers Ltd.) cross a second stile into a fenced off path and continue ahead. Exit through a kissing gate into the lane and turn right. Follow the lane as it bends left, to finally emerge on the A4118 which crosses Fairwood Common. Look out for buzzards on the telegraph wires along this lane - they are frequent visitors here (and so near the poultry farm too).

Cross the main road (carefully) to pick up a track dead ahead, with a recently renovated cottage on the left. The track is signposted to Ilston 1.3 Km. Continue ahead along the track, and, after about 200 yards (182 metres), pass over a stile. In a further 200 yards (182 metres) the path dips down to ford a stream. If this looks a little daunting after rain there is a wooden footbridge on the left. The track starts to ascend gently then swings sharp right, clearly signposted to Ilston, with a gate into Courthouse Farm on the left. Follow the signposted track as it levels off to turn left along a narrow path, again signposted to Ilston. Do not stray off into the fields. At a stile cross over to continue along the path. It may be overgrown in its upper stretch and muddy further on, so take care here. The path widens out to a sunken green lane and gently descends to meet the driveway to The Old Rectory on your left. Turn right here, downhill, passing an old cottage on your right to emerge on the main road through the village of Ilston.

Turn left and follow the road, a small stream flowing past you on your left. Turn left to cross the stream to Ilston church, opposite stables. The turning is marked by a signpost to Kilvrough 1.19Km. Pass through the churchyard to enter Carey's Wood by a kissing gate. Follow the path through the trees, keeping the stream on your right. Cross a small tributary stream coming in from your left (in fact, the one you forded earlier just before Courthouse Farm) and, before you reach a small plantation of tall poplar trees, take a path that continues ahead. The path climbs gently up through the woods ahead. Take care not to follow the path through the poplar plantation - this will take you down the length of Ilston Cwm to Parkmill, and the Gower Inn, about ¾ mile (1.2 km) away (unless this appeals as a lunch break, in which case re-trace your steps to this point and turn right just after the poplars).

Leave the woods over a stile to enter a field, with four prominent oak trees on your right. Cross the field in a straight line to make for a stile opposite. Cross into a second field and continue ahead to a further stile by a gate. The large farm on your right is Kilvrough Farm, hosting some rather cacophonous geese!

Cross the stile into the road (your second and last encounter with the A4118) and turn left. This road can be busy so it is suggested that you cross it here to face oncoming traffic, and keep young children on a tight rein. Continue along the road for about 300 yards (275 metres). Opposite a restored limekiln turn right over a stone stile into a field. Keep to the hedge on your left and where it turns sharp left after about 50 yards (46 metres) do likewise. Continue along the hedge to a stile. Cross the stile into a road (watch out for traffic coming from the left) and make for a kissing gate next to the right of two gates directly opposite.

Pass through the gate and turn immediately left along the field edge, keeping the hedge on your left. Cross the stile into the next field and aim for a stile diagonally opposite. Cross the stile and, keeping the hedge on your right, cross two more stiles to emerge at a final stile. Cross this to emerge in the middle of the bungalows in Beaufort Drive. Continue ahead to meet Kittle Hill Lane. Turn right and return to the start.

Points of Interest:

1. Kittle (originally Kite Hill - apparently where Swansea folk flew their kites at one time) is a small village to the west of Bishopston, and separated from it to the south by Bishopston Valley. Apart from being the start and end of the walk, there is little here to detain you, except perhaps for the Beaufort Arms, a quaint and pleasant pub of some antiquity. It dates from circa 1460, or so it is proudly pronounced around the front door.

2. Ilston, at roughly the halfway point, is an isolated little hamlet, surrounded by acres of peace and quiet. You almost feel afraid to sneeze here, such is the air of tranquility. The Welsh name for the village is Llanilltud Ferwallt, connecting it to St Illtud after whom the church is dedicated. Incidentally, this is the same Illtud after which Llantwit Major (Llanilltud Fawr) in the Vale of Glamorgan gained its name. The existing church building mainly originates from the 13th century, although it is widely believed this was a Christian cell for

long before then. The original building was considered to consist of just the tower, in the form of a transept, and the chancel. The nave is believed to be a later addition during the 15th century, when the hunting area of Parc le Breos was turned over to agriculture, with a corresponding increase in the local population.

The Serpent and the Seagull
(Rhossili - Mewslade - Rhossili)

Access: The walk starts and ends in the village of Rhossili. Leave Swansea through Bishopston, pass through Kittle, and take the road to Parkmill. Continue through Parkmill to Scurlage. Turn right at Scurlage and follow the road to Rhossili.

Start/Parking: Car park in Rhossili. At the time of writing the 'all day' charge is £1.50, although wet, windy, winter week-ends seem to keep the attendant at home. In fact, charges only apply from March to end of October. Grid ref. 415880

Distance/Grade: About 3 miles (4.8 km). Easy; a pleasant stroll, especially during a summer evening.

Terrain: The walk covers grassy paths, clifftops, field paths and lanes.

Facilities: The Worms Head Hotel is just across a lane from the start, and there are loos at the bottom of the car park and a shop at the top. Also at the bottom is the National Trust Visitor Centre and Shop, well worth visiting.

Note: If you intend to venture out onto the Worm itself, carefully read the notices posted in both the National Trust Visitor Centre and Shop window and the old coastguard lookout hut. These give advice about both tide times and areas best avoided during the bird nesting season.

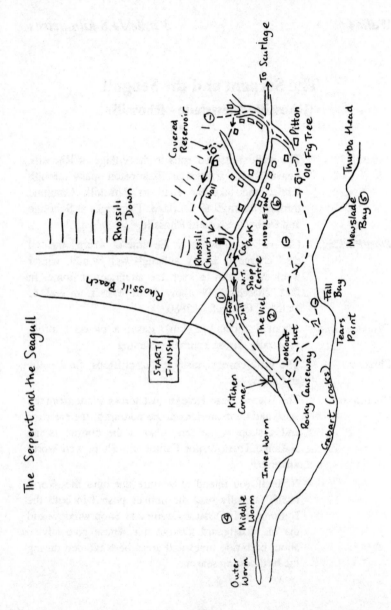

The Serpent and the Seagull

Rhossili Down

Rhossili Beach

Outer Worm

Middle Worm

Inner Worm

Kitchen Corner

Lookout Hut

Rocky Causeway

Crabart (rocks)

Tears Point

Fall Bay

Mewslade Bay

Thurba Head

START/FINISH

Shore Wall

The Viel

N.T. Shop/ Centre

Rhossili Church

N.T. Car Park

MIDDLETON

Old Fig Tree

Pitton

To Scurlage

Covered Reservoir

Wall

40

The Walk:

Leave the car park by the exit at the Worm's Head end, passing the coastguard cottages and National Trust Visitor Centre and Shop on your left. Pass through a wooden gate onto a broad track making for the Worm, and keeping a stone wall on your left. Keep ahead on this track for about ½ mile (0.8 km), passing the rather bumpy ground on your right, indicating the presence of an old Iron Age fort. Where the track swings to the left alongside the wall continue ahead along a broad grassy sward as far as the old coastguard lookout hut (now used by the Countryside Council for Wales as a visitor centre).

Here turn left and follow the cliff path for about ¾ mile (1.2 km), as it first skirts around Fall Bay and then continues on to Mewslade Bay, just before the prominent headland of Thurba. The lower path leading down to Fall Bay is no longer officially a footpath, being closed off some years ago, so keep to the upper path alongside the field wall.

At the eastern end of Fall Bay, do not turn left over the iron ladder stile. Instead, keep the wall on your left and follow the cliff path as it swings to the right. Continue along the path around the headland towards Mewslade Bay. Where the path splits take the one to the right to gain the best views of the clifftop scenery hereabouts. It eventually joins up with the path alongside the wall further along.

Follow the path as it swings to the left above and alongside the Mew Slade. About 50 yards (46 metres) before it rejoins the main path at the wall turn right down a grassy strip to the bottom of the valley. The path is easily identified by a large fig tree about half way down the slope on the right. On joining the path at the bottom, turn left up the valley. Pass through a gate onto a stony track. Continue ahead to emerge at Pitton Farm, through a second gate.

Turn left, passing some cottages on your left, to emerge at the main road to Rhossili. Cross the road to the lane by the post box, ahead and slightly to the right. Continue up the lane to the point where it splits into two tracks. Take the left track (indicated by a waymark arrow on the telegraph pole) and ascend gently. Pass a bungalow on your left, followed by a house on your right. About 50 yards (46 metres) past the house cross over a stile on the left, indicated by a waymark arrow, and a 'Glamorgan Naturalists Trust - Nature Reserve' sign (a body now more correctly known as the Glamorgan Wildlife Trust). The path here is a little overgrown, but never in doubt. Pass an old thatched cottage on your left, and leave the reserve over a stile. Turn half right to join an old overgrown brick driveway. Continue to a stile to the right of a gate. Cross the stile into a lane and aim for the track directly in front of you.

Follow the track to a Welsh Water reservoir. Immediately past the reservoir turn left and aim for the white house ahead, and slightly to the left. Just past the house, pick up a stone wall (not literally) and follow it, keeping it on your left and staying on the common. Do not cross a waymarked stile over the wall but stay on the common, and keep to the right of it. Where it turns sharp left, above Rhossili, continue ahead for about 20 yards (18 metres) to join the wide and grassy path coming off Rhossili Down. Turn left, downhill, onto the path. At the bottom, pass through a kissing gate and continue down the lane to join the main road through Rhossili. Turn right and return to the car park, either via St Mary's Church, or down the road.

Points of Interest:

1. Half way along the cliff walk between Rhossili and the old coastguard lookout station, you will notice some rather lumpy ground to your right. This is all that remains of an old iron-age fort, known as Old Castle. Ravaged both by time and the activities of the local quarrymen it is now only discernible as a series of humps and trenches.

2. On the opposite side of the track, and over the stone wall, is 'The Viel', (or 'The Vile'), this being old Gower for a field. The Viel is one of the few remaining clear examples of the medieval open field strip system. The idea was that the local farmers would have strips of land allocated to them from different areas to ensure all had their fair share of the 'good' and the 'not so good' quality land.

3. Just along from here and below the old coastguard lookout is the rather curiously and quaintly named Kitchen Corner. The wooden hut at the bottom of the cliffs was built by a Swansea fisherman, by the

name of Mr. Coonan, to allow him to fish for bass off the cliff edge, as well as launch his boat. A path leads safely down to it should you wish to explore at closer quarters.

4. The Worm's Head is a fantastic promontory in three clear and distinct sections; the Inner, Middle and Outer Heads, very similar in profile to a serpent. Accessible only around low tide, it is owned by the National Trust and is a haven for sea birds, such as kittiwakes, guillemots, razorbills, and gulls of different types. If you intend to venture across to the Worm make a careful note of tide times displayed at the National Trust shop at Rhossili. It is generally considered safe 2½ hours either side of low tide. Also be aware that some parts of the Worm are sensitive during nesting season. This, too, is publicised. At all other times the trip out to the Outer Head can seem pretty epic, especially in high seas with the waves crashing against the cliffs and the hissing and booming of the sea as it forces its way through the blowhole lower down the cliffside.

5. Mewslade Bay is one of those beaches, along with Fall Bay just before it, that completely disappears at high tide. It is a popular and safe bathing beach. The origin of the name is uncertain but is popularly believed to be derived from the old word 'Mew', meaning a seagull. The dramatic limestone cliffs hereabouts make this a favourite spot for rock climbers. They are also home to colonies of seabirds, in particular, kittiwakes who have bred very successfully here since the 1940s. The word 'slade' seems to mean a dry grassy valley running down to the sea, usually cloaked in gorse, or furze. Have a look at the map to pick out all the slades along this coast.

6. Middleton is the birthplace of Petty Officer Edgar Evans of Scott's ill fated Antarctic expedition. His poigniant memorial is to be seen inside Rhossili church. Middleton was also home to some of the infamous smugglers of Gower, although to walk through it now, you might never think so. Back in the last century the village boasted three inns, including The Ship Inn, now Ship Cottage. It is said they all had more than one cellar too!

Into the Woods

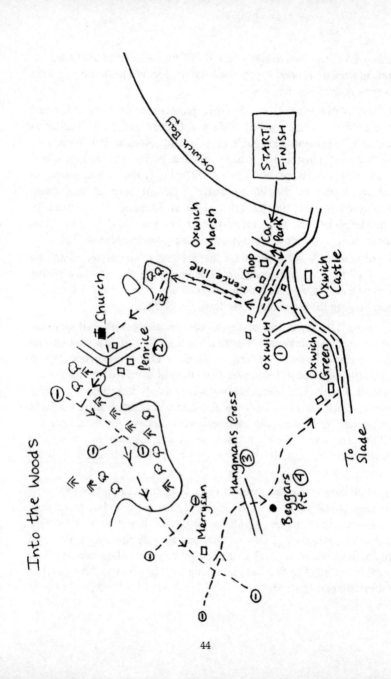

START/FINISH

Oxwich Bay

Oxwich Marsh

Car Park

Fence line

Shop

Church

Penrice

Oxwich Castle

OXWICH ②

①

Oxwich Green ①

Hangmans Cross ③

Beggars Pit ④

Merryfun

To Slade

44

Into the Woods
(Oxwich - Penrice - Oxwich)

Access: The walk starts and ends in the village of Oxwich.
                   Leave Swansea through Bishopston, pass through
                   Kittle, and take the road to Parkmill. Continue
                   through Parkmill and Penmaen as far as the Oxwich
                   turn, by 'The Towers'. Turn left down to the village
                   and look for the car park clearly signposted on the
                   left

Start/Parking: Car park in Oxwich. At the time of writing the 'all
                   day' charge is £2.50 between March and October,
                   although the attendant is also tempted out during
                   winter if the weather is sunny enough. Grid ref.
                   502864

Distance/Grade: About 4 miles (6.4 kilometres). Moderate; a gentle
                   ascent through the woods to Penrice and a bit of a
                   sharp descent at Oxwich but nothing to worry about.

Terrain: The walk covers footpaths and tracks both across
                   fields and through woodland. A number of green
                   lanes are walked on the return leg and these can be
                   muddy. There is also some lane walking.

Facilities: The Oxwich Bay Hotel is close to the car park, and
                   there are loos and a shop nearby.

The Walk:

At the obvious cross-roads in Oxwich take the lane leading away from
the sea, and passing the coastguard lockup about 50 yards (46 metres)
ahead on the right. Pass the thatched cottage where John Wesley used

to preach and stay. Continue ahead, ignoring a signposted footpath on the left to 'Oxwich Green 0.35 km'. Take the signposted footpath about 100 yards (91 metres) further on to the right.

Follow the path as it winds its way alongside a tall garden fence on the right, to finally emerge at the bottom of a field. Continue ahead along the field edge, keeping a fenced off woodland to your right. Cross two ditches, marking field boundaries, to a stile into woods at the bottom right corner of the third field.

Cross the stile (donated by the local branch of the Ramblers Association in 1994) and turn left, into woodland, up a vague path. There is a narrow stream running down the hillside on your left. Continue along the path as it gently winds its way uphill through the woods to emerge at a stile. Cross the stile into a field and trend left along some tractor tracks. Keeping the top edge of the field to your left continue ahead to a stile in the top corner. Cross the stile into a green lane. About ½ way along the lane cross over a gate which is firmly secured to both gateposts by chains and padlocks. (It is hoped to replace this with a stile in the near future.) Emerge from the lane by Penrice Church.

Pass the church on your right and continue ahead to meet the lane passing through the small hamlet. Turn right along the lane, and, at the sharp right hand bend some 100 yards (91 metres) further on, turn left, over a stile, into woods. Follow the path to a junction with a track, looking out for a large pool down on your right. Turn left along the track to meet another track at a junction. Turn left and almost immediately right along a path. Do not go as far as the sharp right hand bend in the track.

Continue along the path through the woods. At a junction, near the boundary with the wood's edge, take the left fork and follow the path through the trees to emerge at a stile. Cross the stile and turn left along the edge of a field. Continue over the stile ahead (or through the gate, if open) into the next field - do not cross the stile to the left. Continue along the edge of the field, with two fences on your left, to leave it over a stile into a green lane.

Turn right, and after 20 yards (18 metres) turn left down another green lane. Continue ahead, passing the remote cottage of 'Merrysun' on your left.

At the next junction just past the house turn left. A well is marked here on the OS Explorer map, and if you listen carefully, you can hear the water gurgling nearby on the right. Follow the green lane (Grave Lane!) until you come to the road that connects Penrice and Horton at Hangman's Cross. Cross the road and take the green lane directly opposite, leaving Hangman's Cross as fast as you feel appropriate. Swing left at Beggar's Pit and continue along the lane. After about ½ mile (0.8 km) the lane emerges at some houses on the lane from Oxwich Green to Slade.

Turn left into the lane and follow it as it continues ahead to Oxwich Green. Pass through the hamlet and about 50 yards past the lane leading to Penrice look for a signposted footpath on the left, (Oxwich 0.35 km) after about 50 yards (46 metres). Pass through a gap in the wall and descend rather steeply to the lane previously encountered at the start of the walk. Turn right down the lane, passing John Wesley's cottage on your left, and continue ahead to the cross roads and the start of the walk.

Points of Interest:

1. Oxwich, believed to be derived from the Scandinavian 'Axwick', meaning a water creek, is a small seaside resort with a large personality, especially during hot summer months. At this time it becomes utterly clogged up with day trippers making for the sands, and rendering parking a nightmare. The 'back of the village', however, remains relatively unfrequented by visitors and is not without its share of interest. John Wesley stayed here on a number of occasions in a cottage in Oxwich main street, marked by a plaque on the cottage wall. Most probably, in his day, and for some time after, all the cottages in Oxwich would have been thatched and whitewashed.

Before tourism arrived here the mainstay of the villagers were quarrying for the local limestone, and the sea. Towards the end of the 19th century many village men set sail with the whaling ships that worked out of Bristol. Today holiday makers provide a considerable proportion of the local income.

2. The peaceful cluster of white houses that make up Penrice to me

sum up what Gower must have looked like back in John Wesley's time. But peaceful it certainly was not, by all accounts. During the early 1700's there was a twice weekly market here, as well as the regular 'Hiring Fairs'. Each was an excuse for celebration with a vengeance, those too drunk to walk being laid out in rows in the nearby village churchyard. The presence of a pub in the village (now long gone) was of little help! The church, which seems to have singularly failed in delivering its message of wholesome living (at least, during the numerous festivities) is dedicated to St. Andrew, and is one of the oldest in Gower. It was built in the 12th century, fairly soon after the Normans arrived in Gower. It has a surprisingly large porch which was probably used as the local school during the last century. Look out to the left, when facing the church door, for the rather sad grave of a local widow, murdered nearby. The inscription reads:

To The Memory

Of

Mary

Wife Of

James Kavanagh of

Penmaen Who Was Murdered By

(left blank)

The 3rd Of October 1829

Aged 75 Years

'Prepare For Death Make No Delay

She In A Moment Was Snatched Away'

The church window, nearby, is also of some interest; look out for the sad and smiling faces on either side of the lintel.

3. Hangman's Cross, also known locally as Cold Comfort, was the last place in the memory of unfortunate sheep stealers as they unceremoniously passed from this world to the next. Not a place to loiter.

4. Sorry, but research into the oddly named Beggar's Pit revealed nothing. I shall continue to dig!

On a Pilgrimage
(Llangenydd - Burry Holms - Llangenydd)

Access: The walk starts and ends at the Hillend car park,
                     Llangenydd. Leave Swansea by Upper Killay, taking
                     the B4271 to Llanrhidian. Continue ahead, through
                     Burry Green, to Llangenydd. Pass through the
                     village to a junction of three lanes. Take the left turn
                     to Hillend caravan and camping site.

Start/Parking: Start from the Hillend main car park, next to the
                     dunes. There is a charge per day of £1.50, applicable
                     from April to October. Grid ref. 413909

Distance/Grade: About 4 miles (6.4 km). Moderate; a superb walk
                     combining a wild and remote beach with some truly
                     dramatic coastal scenery. This is a wild and romantic
                     walk on a dry but windy winter's day, made even
                     better if the tide is out.

Terrain: The outward walk covers a sandy beach, some rocks,
                     a coastal dune path, and a length of boardwalk
                     (slippery when wet!). The return is along a green
                     track, with the option of revisiting the beach.

Facilities: Facilities are limited on this walk, by virtue of its
                     remoteness. There is a shop on the Broughton Farm
                     caravan site, en route, but this is closed in winter.
                     During summer months snacks are also available at
                     Hillend.

On a Pilgrimage

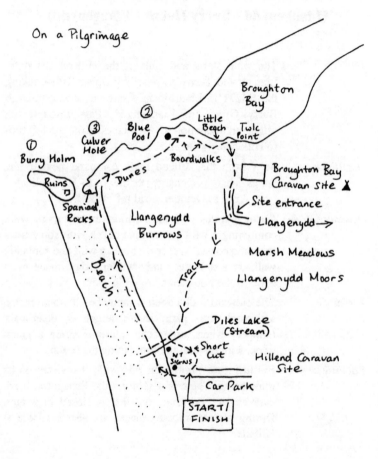

The Walk:

From the car park, take the fenced path leading directly through the sand dunes to emerge on the remote north western end of Rhossili Beach. The beach is owned by the National Trust up as far as Diles Lake, there being a sign to this effect as you leave the dunes. Turn right and walk for about ¾ mile (1.2 km) in the direction of Burry Holms.

On reaching the island it is possible to scale the small cliff to explore it further, but be aware of the tide times. It is considered safe to cross within 2½ hours either side of low tide, and well worth the little extra effort if time permits. Our walk, however, continues by aiming for the right hand corner of the beach, behind some low rocks. Look for a well defined path heading up right into the dunes, almost level with the ruins of the Hermitage on the Holms. It starts just before a small but easily identified grassy tump. Follow the path as it first ascends the slope, and then turns left to level off and follow the edge of the dunes, overlooking the sandy bays below.

Keep with the path as it winds its way through the dunes above the bays. Look out behind you for a passage through the rock, known as the Three Chimneys, visible at low tide. This is on the western edge of Bluepool Bay. A little further on, a narrow path winds down to the left from a spot marked by a sign warning of the dangerous nature of the terrain, to the Blue Pool itself, on the opposite side of the bay. Be aware that when the tide is in, this path is the only way off the bay! The terrain hereabouts is only dangerous if you ignore safety signs. The path to Blue Pool does require some care, and involves a bit of a step up at the start on the return up the hill. If you do venture down to the bay, and pass through The Chimneys you will find the Culver Hole cave (not to be confused with the Port Eynon Culver Hole).

Continue on towards Broughton Bay. Alongside the bay, as the path curves around inland towards the caravan site, the path has been 'boardwalked' to minimise erosion. Be very careful here after rain; the wooden slats are very slippery and would do Torvill and Dean proud!

At the end of the boardwalk turn right along the tarmaced access road following waymarks to exit the caravan site. If in doubt and feeling hemmed in by caravans just ask for the way out!

At the entrance/exit to the site turn right along a track by the main site sign, keeping a hedge on your left. Cross over a stile by a gate and continue ahead, in the direction of Rhossili Down. Ignore a stile on your left but keep ahead on the track, passing over a further stile. At the obvious stream (Diles Lake) you have a choice. Either cross the stream (no bridge, so wet feet are almost a racing certainty) and continue along the track, or follow the stream to the beach and then turn left, crossing the stream where it fans out onto the beach. If you take the first option the track continues unerringly back to the car park. Note that this is not a definitive right of way but is frequently used by visitors. If, however, you opt to return once more to the beach, look out for the second National Trust sign on your left, at which point, turn left back up the path through the dunes to the car park.

Points of Interest:

1. Burry Holm, Holms or Holmes (place name spelling in Gower is never consistent!), is derived from the old Scandinavian 'Boring Holmr', Holmr meaning island. About ¼ mile long (0.4 km), it is only accessible for about 2½ hours either side of low tide. There are strong associations with the 6th century Saint Cenydd, the ruins of a medieval chapel on the island thought to have been built as a shrine, or site of pilgrimage. It is said that the chapel was constructed by the 11th century hermit, Caradog, who lived on Burry Holm.

2. The Blue Pool is a natural, circular pool in the rocks of Bluepool Bay. It measures about 15 feet (4.5 metres) across and can be up to 15 feet deep, depending on what the tide has managed to leave behind. It is in this area that about 200 years ago, the first of a number of gold coins were found embedded in nearby rocks. Finds occurred right up to about 1840, when some locals took it upon themselves to blow up the rocks with gunpowder. At that point they were forcibly prevented from creating any further havoc by the local squire, no coins being documented as found since then. Keep your eyes open, and keep me posted!

3. About 100 yards (91 metres) west of Bluepool Bay is the second of Gower's two Culver Holes, near the passageway through the rock. A

large quantity of human bones and shards of pottery dating back to the Bronze Age have been discovered here, leading archaeologists to believe it was a place of burial rather than a dwelling. It was also the site of a failed attempt to hide smuggled contraband. Take care if exploring the cave; it is only accessible at low tide, and you run the risk of being cut off.

A Hop to Frog Moor

To Burry Green

To Reynoldston A4118

Cadiz Hall

Geranium Cottage and Paddock

Frogmoor Farm

Frog Moor

Boggy ground!

gate

Burry Farm

Garage

Stream

School

KNELSTON

Closed off Green Lane

Stile back into Green Lane

Fields

START/FINISH

To Bury

To Scurlage A4118

54

A Hop to Frog Moor
(Knelston - Frog Moor - Knelston)

Access:

The walk starts and ends in the village of Knelston. Leave Swansea through Bishopston, pass through Kittle and take the road through Parkmill. Continue along the main South Gower road, to Knelston.

Start/Parking:

Parking is limited in Knelston so wherever you park, be sensitive to the needs of the locals. There is limited parking near the start of the walk. Pass through Knelston and look for a converted chapel on the right, about 200 yards (183 metres) past the school (also on the right). Take the next right turn signposted to Stoney Forge B&B, just past a post-box on the left, and park on the left opposite three houses. The lane is a dead-end, but has a footpath sign showing 'Burry 1.68Km'. Grid ref. 466890.

(Note that at weekends and school holidays it should be possible to park in the pull-in in front of Knelston School).

Distance/Grade: About 4 miles (6.4 kilometres). Moderate; this is a level stroll, requiring little effort other than good eyesight to seek out the yellow waymark arrows.

Terrain:

The walk covers fields, lanes, and a short stretch of moorland. It is not recommended after a period of rain. One stretch of path is rather overgrown, so bring your pruners!

Facilities:

There is a garage shop in Knelston, which is very well stocked. Other than that there is nothing else.

The Walk:

From the start, cross a stile on your left into a field. Do not continue ahead up the green lane - it is blocked off further up. Turn immediately right to follow the edge of the field, keeping the hedge on your right. The path keeps parallel to the (disused) green lane, crossing over stiles at every hedge line. At the far right corner of the eighth field cross a stile to re-enter the green lane. Take care here, the step down into the lane is higher than encountered thus far. Turn left down the lane (rather overgrown at first) and continue to a tarmac lane. This is the lane connecting Llandewi to Burry.

Cross the lane to a track ahead, cross the stream over either of two bridges and turn right along the track. (Do not cross the stile into the field ahead. A footpath is marked on the map in our direction but is fenced off further along.) Continue ahead, passing firstly a farm and then two cottages, all on your left. After the cottages cross a stile into a grassy paddock. Keep to the left edge of the paddock and cross a stile in the top left corner. Cross the next stile in front and turn half right, to follow a waymark arrow, painted on the corner of a stone wall. Continue ahead across the field to another stile.

From here the path seems to run out, there being no further stiles or waymark arrows. However, keep ahead and leave the field via a gate straight ahead. (Ignore the gate on the right.) Turn left, uphill slightly, to leave by a gate. Turn right, and then continue ahead, keeping the hedge on your left. Where the hillside starts to gently slope to the right keep ahead and look for a cottage, ahead and right. Descend to the cottage (Geranium Cottage) and pass through the gate into the back yard. Pass through the yard to join a lane through a gate.

Turn right and continue down the lane to Burry Farm, on a junction with a 'No Through Road', off to the left. Turn left, up the 'No Through Road', and follow it right to the end, a distance of ½ mile (0.8 km). Pass two houses on your left and one on your right. At the end of the lane, with a cottage on your right and two gates in front of you, cross the stile to your left, and trend right to meet the track coming from the nearest of the two gates. You are now on the edge of Frog Moor.

Turn left along the track and follow it as far as 'The Cottage', all but hidden by a tall surrounding hedge. Turn right down a vague track, evident by tractor tracks across the moor, and continue ahead towards fields. This track meets the end of a tarmac lane, but a stream has to be crossed first! Step carefully! Turn left onto the lane and pass through a gate. Continue on down the lane as it passes Frogmoor Farm on the left. Finally the lane emerges in Knelston, almost opposite the petrol garage. Turn right and walk back to where you started.

(There is a path marked on the OS map, making a shortcut from the lane into Knelston, passing the remains of Knelston Old Church. On the ground neither the start nor the end of the path are obvious).

Points of Interest:

1. Knelston is a small village that straggles along the main road. It is of no immediate interest, but does possess some strong links with the past. The ruins of an ancient church, behind the school, are dedicated to St Taurin. They are not particularly easy to find. There are also a number of standing stones in the fields hereabouts.

2. Cadiz Hall, near Geranium Cottage, whilst not directly on the route, is very near it. The name conjures up all sorts of Spanish imagery, but is a bit of a let down, an inadvertent con, almost. According to Wynford Vaughan Thomas the name is no more than a corruption of Cady, or Cade, a family well established in Gower during the Middle Ages, owning land on and around the western slopes of Cefn Bryn. The date of the house is believed to be from around 16th century.

3. The wonderfully named Frog Moor is a rather bleak tract of open land, covered for the most part in bracken and gorse, to the west of Cefn Bryn.

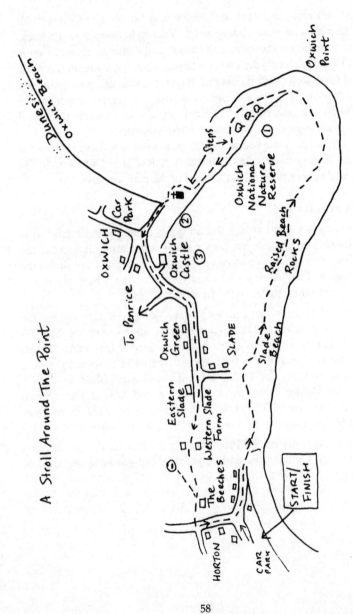

A Stroll Around The Point

Dunes Beach
Oxwich Beach
Oxwich Point
Steps
① Oxwich National Nature Reserve
OXWICH
Car Park
② Oxwich Castle
③
To Penrice
Oxwich Green
Raised Beach
Rocks
Eastern Slade
Western Slade Farm
Slade
Slade Beach
The Beeches
HORTON
CAR PARK
START/FINISH

A Stroll around the Point
(Horton - Oxwich - Horton)

Access: The walk starts and ends in the village of Horton. Leave Swansea through Bishopston, pass through Kittle and take the road through Parkmill. Continue along the main South Gower road, passing through Knelston and Scurlage, towards Port Eynon. Turn left at Moor Corner Farm, about ½ mile (0.8 kilometre) past Scurlage. Take the next right turn, signposted to Horton.

Start/Parking: 'Pay and Display' car park on sea front near Horton Beach, behind the sand dunes. At the time of writing the 'all day' charge is £2.30, payable between April 1st and September 30th. Grid ref. 475875

Distance/Grade: About 6 miles (9.6 kilometres). Moderate; there is one short, sharp pull up steps cut into the hillside in the Oxwich National Nature Reserve just before a further stepped descent down to Oxwich Church.

Terrain: The walk covers coastal paths, fields, woodlands, green lanes and tarmac lanes.

Facilities: There is a shop (The Shipwreckers) in Horton village, (closed during the 'off season') and loos at the car park. Refreshments are also available at the Oxwich Bay Hotel, in Oxwich, about two thirds of the way around.

The Walk:

Leave the car park by its entrance, and with your back to the sea, turn right along the road. After 100 yards (91 metres), and where the road swings left uphill, turn half right, down a tarmac lane signposted to 'Sea Beach Nursing Home'. Continue ahead along the lane to pass a row of houses on your left, including the Nursing Home. Where the lane ends turn half right down a footpath, signposted Oxwich 2.3 km, and initially hemmed in by tall hedges either side. After about 70 yards (63 metres) cross a rather dilapidated stile and continue along the path.

Soon the path emerges onto a broad grassy shelf, with fields on your left and a rocky drop to the sea on your right. Cross a number of fairly recently constructed stiles, all with dog passes built into them. This part of the walk takes you along a 'raised beach', the cliffs up on the left forming the previous tideline of many years ago. Look out here in spring for both the early purple orchid and the short pink spring squill.

After about 2½ miles (4 km) the path rounds the headland of Oxwich Point to enter a signposted national nature reserve. The reserve takes the form of a mile long (1.6 km) stretch of woodland overlooking Oxwich Bay. Follow the path through the woodland, as it offers tantalising glimpses across the bay of the Great Tor and Three Cliffs Bay on the far side of the Oxwich sands. The path soon rises up a steep set of steps cut out of the hillside. Contour the hillside near its top for a few hundred yards before descending, again fairly steeply, down more steps. At the bottom turn left to pass by the little church of St Illtud, on your left. (The church is well worth closer scrutiny but, be aware that the door may be locked.) The path becomes a lane where it meets the church gate. Continue ahead along this lane, to pass the Oxwich Bay Hotel on your left and the beach on your right.

When you come to the obvious crossroads, about 200 yards (183 metres) past the Hotel, turn left to ascend the hill leading to the small hamlet of Oxwich Green. Towards the top of the hill, look for a grassy lane leading off left to Oxwich Castle. It is well worth a quick 'there and back' to see what was once the home of the powerful Mansel family in the 16th century. Look out especially for the remarkable dovecote.

Returning to the lane, known rather quaintly as Ganderstreet, turn left and continue to Oxwich Green. Continue along the lane, through the village, ignoring tempting little tracks sneaking off to your left. Where the lane ends, continue ahead along a farm track towards Western Slade Farm. Walk through the farmyard, keeping the barns on your left and the farmhouse on your right. Look for a gate and stile marked 'Horton' on the far side of the farmyard and cross here into a field. Keeping the hedge on your left continue ahead along the edge of the field to a stile dead ahead, beside a large animal drinking trough. Cross over the stile into a second field and continue ahead, this time keeping the hedge on your right. When the hedge runs out on you, bear slightly to your right and make for the solitary house ahead. Pass through a gate into a stony lane, keeping the house on your left.

Continue ahead down the lane to meet the road coming down the hill into Horton. Turn left here and follow the road downhill. Round the sharp right hand bend at the bottom of the hill, and retrace your steps back to the car park on your left.

Points of Interest:

1. The woodland nature reserve at Oxwich plays host to a remarkable variety of wild flowers, especially in May and June. Keep an eye out for ramsons, or wild garlic, (difficult to miss on account of their oniony odour) and bluebells, both in profusion. But look out as well for the less common but aptly named stinking hellebore, which flowers around April time, the blue gromwell, which flowers from May to June and the Herb Paris. These plants thrive on the calcium rich limestone found all around the Gower coastline.

2. The little church of St. Illtud is of 13th construction, built on an older site dating back as far as the 6th century. It is easy to miss from Oxwich village, being hidden away in the woods. If the door is open take a peep inside. The ancient font is alleged to have been brought here by St Illtud himself. Also in the churchyard is a war grave dedicated to an unknown sailor who was washed up hereabouts during the First World War. It is possibly the loneliest war grave in the country.

3. The imposing castle near Oxwich Green was built back in 14th century for the Norman de la Mare family. It later passed into the hands of the Mansels, who largely rebuilt it in the 16th century to its present proportions. More of a fortified mansion than a castle it has recently undergone fairly extensive renovation, including the rather impressive and very visible dovecot, or pigeon house. This would have provided a steady supply of fresh meat throughout the year, but especially so during the winter months. In 1557, one Anne Mansel, an incumbent of the castle, was killed here by a stray stone during a local brawl whilst trying to calm down a potential riot. This all came to a head over plunder rights to a ship grounded in Oxwich Bay. The original claimant to the plunder, Sir George Herbert of Swansea, who led the rabble that marched on the castle, was arrested and taken to court by the Mansels. He was found guilty of affray (but apparently not of murder), fined heavily and ordered to hand over the cargo of the stricken ship to the Mansels.

The castle is administered by Cadw, but is, unfortunately, closed during the winter months, during which time it has to be admired from over a nearby gate. It reopens on May 1st each year.

A Trip to the Lighthouse
(Llanmadoc - Whiteford Burrows - Llanmadoc)

Access: The walk starts and ends in the village of
                   Llanmadoc. Leave Swansea through Gowerton and
                   pass through Penclawdd, Llanrhidian and Cheriton.
                   Continue on to Llanmadoc, passing the Britannia Inn
                   on your right. Keep ahead and turn right down a hill
                   immediately before Llanmadoc Church. Look for a
                   car park in a field about 100 yards (91 metres) down
                   the hill, on the right.

Start/Parking: Car park in field, privately owned and with an
                   honesty box. At the time of writing there is a 50p 'all
                   day' charge. Grid ref. 439935.

Distance/Grade: About 4 miles (6.4 kilometres). Moderate; more or
                   less flat all the way, apart from one optional short,
                   steep pull. There is an additional flat stretch which
                   adds a further 2 miles (3.2 kilometres), if you decide
                   to cover it. The extra effort is amply rewarded, and
                   well recommended. (Do it!)

Terrain: The walk covers sand dunes, beaches, cinder tracks,
                   woodland paths and tarmac roads. Note that there are
                   warning notices regarding unexploded shells, left
                   from artillery practice during World War II, along
                   Whiteford Sands, so do not pick up any metal
                   objects you may come across, either in the dunes or
                   on the beach. Locals tell me there have never been
                   any untoward incidents here - I vote we keep it that
                   way!

A Trip To The Lighthouse

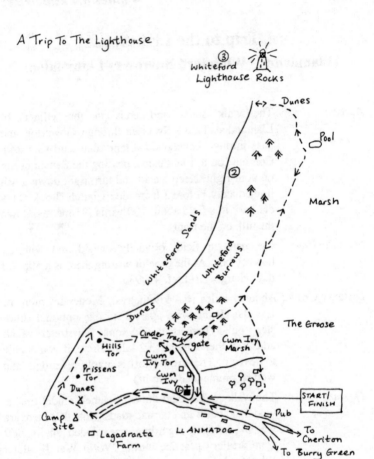

③ Whiteford Lighthouse Rocks

Dunes

Pool

②

Marsh

Whiteford Sands

Whiteford Burrows

Dunes

The Groose

Cinder Track — gate

Hills Tor

Cwm Ivy Marsh

Cwm Ivy Tor

Prissens Tor

Cwm Ivy

Dunes

START/FINISH

Camp Site

Pub

Lagadranta Farm

LLANMADOG

To Cheriton

To Burry Green

Facilities: The Britannia Inn is near the start/end of the walk, but nothing else. Although toilets are passed in the field leading to Broughton Beach, they are strictly for the use of campers and are not public facilities.

The Walk:

Leave the car park and turn left up the hill towards Llanmadoc Church. Take the lane to the right running alongside the church and follow it for about 1 mile (1.6 km) to a camp site. There are two sites along the lane but this one is where the road runs out at Lagadranta Farm.

Turn right down a permissive track through the centre of the campsite, and continue ahead, to meet the wall of sand dunes separating the site from Broughton Bay. At the dunes, turn either left or right, to follow a sandy path on to the beach. Once on the beach turn right, to make for the rocky promontory of Prissen's Tor. Note that some maps and guidebooks also call this Spritsail Tor. This is the dividing line between Broughton Bay and Whiteford Sands. At low tide it can be rounded with ease, but at high tide you may have to scramble over the rocks. This is not difficult.

Continue along the beach to pass Hills Tor, on your right. Once round Hills Tor continue along the beach keeping the dunes on your right until you are level with Cwm Ivy Tor, the large and obvious rock tower on your right. Cwm Ivy Tor is marked on the Explorer Map but not the Landranger Map, but you would be pretty hard pressed to miss it! Look for a clear sandy path through the dunes, immediately before and to the right of a pinewood plantation, leading inland to the base of the Tor.

Once near the foot of the Tor, pass over a stile and turn left onto a cinder track. (For the energetic, it is perfectly possible, from here, to execute a nimble 'there and back' to the summit of the Tor. The rewards for this burst of energy are in the form of stunning views, both of Whiteford Sands spread out below your feet, and of pretty well the whole of the walk).

Having turned left, continue along the track, passing the plantation on your left. Where it comes to an end, pass through a wooden gate on your left (the smaller of the two, with a rather faded National Trust oak leaf motif barely discernible). Continue along a cinder track, passing a small bungalow on your left. The track skirts the landward side of the plantation, passing between some beautiful pines, planted here some 40 to 50 years ago, by the then owner. This whole area is now owned by the National Trust.

Where the plantation ends, pass through a gateway, and, about 50 yards (45 metres) later, turn right through a swing gate to walk along the top of the Sea Wall.

(To extend the walk by a further 2 miles (3.2 km), it is possible, and highly recommended, to continue ahead here towards the beach on an obvious and signposted track. After about ½ mile (0.8 km) the track swings to the left, identifiable by a prominent grassy dune on the left of the split. Ignore this and, instead, continue ahead, and slightly right, along a narrower path. This eventually leads through further plantations, past a pool on your right and onto the sands and Whiteford Lighthouse. Return by the way you came, making a careful note of where you emerge on the beach).

Continue along the top of the Sea Wall, as you make your way inland. To your left are the Llanrhidian salt marshes, to your right the reclaimed meadows of Cwm Ivy Marsh. Where the Sea Wall ends, pass over a stile and take the track that leads ahead and uphill. Ignore a path that leads off to the right into the woods. Stay with the track, as it passes two remotely situated cottages, to climb gently to the village of Llanmadoc. If thirst and hunger have brought you to your knees, the Britannia Inn is about 100 yards (91 metres) down the main road on the left, through the village.

Otherwise, turn right along the road, to arrive back at Llanmadoc Church. Turn right down the hill just before the church, to return to the car park.

Points of Interest:

1. Llanmadoc Church, built in the 13th century, lies on the site of a sixth century shrine dedicated to St. Madoc, or Madog. It is believed that Madoc was a student of St Cenydd, after whom the village of Llangenydd is named. The church was extensively restored by the

Victorians in the 1860's but still retains its charm and beauty, as well as its reputation for being the smallest church in Gower. Inside can be found an early Romano-Celtic stone bearing the inscription 'Guan son of Duectus lies here'. The stone was discovered in 1862 built into the wall of the Old Rectory.

2. Whiteford Burrows have been documented as being named after the Scandinavian, 'Hvit's Fjord', although another story tells us the name Whitford (as it is also known) derives from the crossing, or ford, of St Whit (any connection with Whitland, I wonder?). The Burrows are an extensive expanse of pine plantations, beach and sand dunes, especially rich in plant and animal life, and are regarded by many as being the remotest and wildest part of Gower. They were bought by the National Trust in 1965. The pines are home to kestrels, and there is a rumour of peregrine falcons hereabouts. Off the sands will be found cormorants, shags, oystercatchers and turnstones, the latter two leaving a 'trademark' of neatly opened, and otherwise undamaged, shells.

From May to September there is a rich carpet of flowers, including bloody cranesbill, vipers bugloss, ragwort and knapweed. Around July The Groose, that part of the Llanrhidian Marshes held back by the Sea Wall, (constructed in 1638) opens up into a sea of pale blue coloured sea lavender and pink marsh mallow. A little earlier, in May/June, the orchids and flag iris are both at their best, the irises particularly so within the confines of the Cwm Ivy Marsh, the 'reclaimed' land.

3. The rather elegant old lighthouse at Whiteford Point is no longer in use, other than as a handy roost for cormorants. It is possibly the only Victorian cast iron lighthouse still in situ. Its date of origin is unclear; claims for 1854 and 1865 being put forward, but its decommission date of 1933 is certain. Moves are now afoot to restore and maintain it. In the meantime it stands as a stern reminder of just how treacherous the sea can be in these parts. In 1868, sixteen out of a total of nineteen ships, outward bound from the port of Llanelli, were wrecked on the same tide just off the sands of Broughton Beach, with a loss of 30 lives.

A Walk Through History

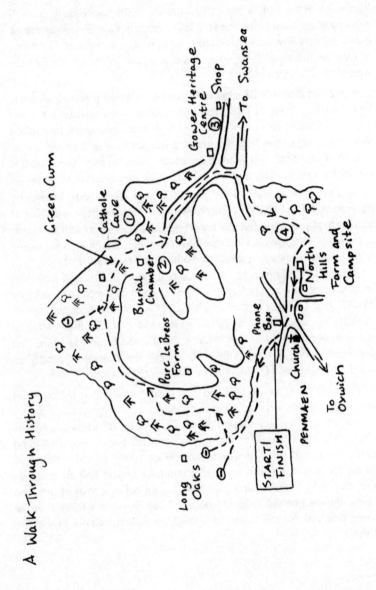

Green Cum

Cathole Cave ①

Gower Heritage Centre ③ Shop

To Swansea

Burial Chamber ②

④

North Hills Farm and Campsite

Parc le Breos Farm

Phone Box

Penmaen Church

To Oxwich

Long Oaks

START/FINISH

A Walk through History
(Penmaen - Green Cwm - Penmaen)

Access: The walk starts and ends in the village of Penmaen. Leave Swansea through Bishopston, pass through Kittle, and take the road to Parkmill. Continue through Parkmill and take a right turn in Penmaen village, by the church.

Start/Parking: National Trust car parking area, about 100 yards (91 metres) up the lane from the church, on the right. Grid ref. 532887

Distance/Grade: About 3½ miles (5.6 km). Moderate; a bit of a pull up through Northill Woods, but nothing serious.

Terrain: The walk covers woodland tracks, a wooded valley, bridleways and country lanes.

Facilities: There is a good café at the restored mill in Parkmill, ('Y Felin Ddwr' - Gower Heritage Centre, at which walkers are warmly welcomed) and a well stocked shop about 100 yards (91 metres) further into the village (Shepherd's). Both are at the foot of Green Cwm.

The Walk:

From the car parking area turn to the north along the obvious track away from the lane, passing two cottages on your right. Do not take the track that curves off to the right just after the parking area, but continue ahead to the perimeter fence of Coed Abertawe (Abertawe Woods) clearly signposted by a gate.

Do not enter the woods at this point but turn left along a path under a tunnel of trees, keeping the forestry boundary fence on your right. Stay with the path as it faithfully follows the forest edge for about ½ mile (0.8 km). The path then joins a broad track coming in from the left. Turn right along the track and follow it for a short distance to a stile and gate on your right, just before the track divides.

Enter the forest through the gate, or over the stile, passing a forestry commission signpost on your right. Follow the path which after a short distance broadens out to a track. Keep ahead on the track as it slowly turns back on the direction you have come from Penmaen. Gradually descend for about ¾ mile (1.2 km) to meet the wooded valley bottom of Green Cwm.

Where the track meets the bottom of the Cwm at an obvious junction, turn right onto another track. Continue ahead along the grassy bottom of this delightful and secluded valley, hemmed in by steep wooded slopes on either side. Pass the high limestone crag up on your left, into which runs the Cathole cave, soon followed by the 'Giant's Grave', in the valley bottom on your right.

Pass through a gate out of the meadow and turn half left to join a tarmac lane as it takes you to the mouth of the valley at Parkmill. After about ½ mile (0.8 km) you will come to a ford through the Green Cwm stream. Do not cross the ford or the footbridge next to it, unless you want to visit the Gower Heritage Centre or Shepherd's. (If you do, retrace your steps to this point.) Instead, turn right along a lane, passing a cottage on your right, and an outhouse on the left. After about 100 yards (91 metres), cross (carefully) the main A4118 road, and pass through a gateway directly opposite, and marked by a bridleway signpost.

Take care not to continue ahead along a footpath here, but instead, turn half right and follow the bridleway as it gently ascends through Northill Wood, parallel to the main road on your right. As you emerge from the wood, pass through a gate and continue ahead along the track. It soon narrows to a path. The path meets the end of a tarmac lane at the point where the lane enters a caravan site.

Continue ahead along the lane to finally emerge back on the main road crossed earlier. (Take care to keep to the lane, and not accidentally wander into the forecourt of Northill Farm holiday cottages.) Cross the road and walk up the lane opposite, keeping the church on your left, to arrive back at the start.

Points of Interest:

1. The Cathole (or Cat's Hole) is clearly seen from the track leading along the bottom of Green Cwm, high up in a limestone tower on the left, about 300 yards (274 metres) after joining the track. It can be easily reached if you want to explore more closely. Archaeological excavations were carried out in 1955 and again in 1968, revealing evidence of man's occupation in the form of a number of flint blades, dating back to around 12,000BC.

2. A further 200 yards (182 metres) down the Cwm is the spectacular 'Giant's Grave', a megalithic tomb, or cromlech, dating from about 3,500 BC. It was first properly excavated by Lord Avebury in 1869, revealing the remains of about 25 people. Until a further excavation in 1937, conducted by Professor Glyn Daniel, it was believed that the tomb was circular. It can be clearly seen today that it is, in fact, quite elongated, and almost heart shaped. It is believed that when the site was originally constructed it would have been by the bank of the stream which now flows under this stretch of Green Cwm, emerging further down the valley. The site seems to be variously known as the 'Giant's Grave', Parc le Breos burial chamber and Parc le Bruce burial chamber.

3. The Park Mill, after which Parkmill earns its name, has now been well restored as a tourist attraction and is featured as a part of the Gower Heritage Centre. Although the original mill was used to grind flour the water from the stream was also harnessed to power the sawmill.

4. The bridleway up through the Northill Woods, and leading back to Penmaen, was the original main road (if road is an appropriate term) before it was replaced by the present route up the hill to its right at the beginning of the last century. This might give us an insight into how truly remote and difficult of access Gower must have been in those far-off days!

To The Smugglers' Beach

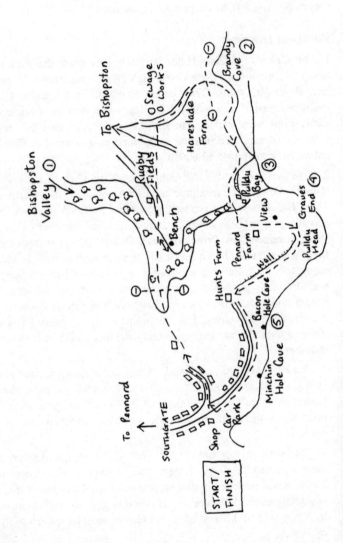

To the Smugglers' Beach
(Southgate - Bishopston - Southgate)

Access:	The walk starts and ends in the village of Southgate, near Pennard. Leave Swansea through Bishopston, pass through Kittle, and take the road to Pennard. Do not take the turning to Parkmill but continue on to Pennard. Pass the golf course on your right and keep on the main road through the village until you come to the end of the road (Southgate Terminus) and a car park.
Start/Parking:	Car park in Southgate run by the National Trust. At the time of writing there is a charge of £1.50 from March to October. From November to February the car park is free. Grid ref. 554874
Distance/Grade:	About 5 miles (8 km). Strenuous; on account of both its length and the fairly long uphill stretch out of Pwlldu Bay.
Terrain:	The walk covers coastal paths, green lanes and tarmac roads. Ground covered includes wooded valleys, fields (including a rugby pitch) and coastline, including some exhilarating clifftops.
Facilities:	There is a good general provisions store by the side of the car park at Southgate, but nothing else along the route.

The Walk:

With your back to the sea make for the further of two tarmac lanes ahead. At this second lane, known as Hael Lane, turn right and follow it to a left bend in the road. Continue around the corner and along the lane between houses. After about 500 yards (457 metres) turn right down a signposted bridleway opposite a bungalow.

Follow the bridleway through a gate and pass Hael Farm on your left. Continue straight ahead, passing through a gate. The track here is quite rough and could be wet in winter. When you come to an obvious junction of paths and stiles keep straight ahead, downhill, the bed of a small stream running alongside you on your right. When you reach the bottom of the hill turn left to join a path that runs alongside a river. You are now in Bishopston Valley.

After about 100 yards (91 metres), cross the river by a narrow footbridge on your right. Continue ahead along the path for about 20 yards (18 metres), to pick up a smaller path leading off to the right and uphill. At first the path is a little vague and overgrown, but is readily identifiable by a series of wooden steps at its base. Climb the path, steeply at first, and turn left at the first obvious bend. Take the next path leading off to the right. This arrives at a bench from where there are good views across the Bishopston Valley to Pwlldu Bay in the distance. Do not continue past the bench.

Having taken in the views retrace your steps to the main path and turn right. Where the path splits at a stile after entering woods take the path leading to the right through a gate. Continue ahead along a clear track. Where the track meets a tarmac lane turn left and continue down the lane for about 150 yards (136 metres).

Turn right through a waymarked kissing gate to cross some rough pasture. Turn left into the next field and make directly for a gate in the hedge opposite. If you cannot make out the gate clearly, aim for the tall rugby posts looming over the hedge. Cross the top of the first rugby field and proceed ahead to the second. Pass the rugby clubhouse on your left and continue ahead down a cinder track to a tarmac lane. Cross the lane into a field opposite, over a stile. Follow the path across the field, keeping a tall hedge to your right. At the end of the field you will emerge at another tarmac lane.

Turn right down the lane, passing firstly a house on your right and then a large sewage works on your left (sorry about that!). Keep ahead along the lane which, after a short distance, becomes a track. Where the track ends, at Hareslade Farm down on the right, continue ahead along a path. Keep with the path as it leads you unerringly to the pretty little bay of Brandy Cove.

Leave Brandy Cove by following the lower of the two paths on your right, as you face the sea. Continue along the path as it hugs the coastline for about 1 mile (1.6 km) to arrive at Pwlldu Bay. Keep with the path here until it meets an obvious track descending from the right. Join the track and turn left down towards the beach, to emerge behind a large bank of well rounded, sea washed pebbles. Cross the stream ahead over a footbridge and start to climb the path into a woodland.

At a squeeze gate on your right turn sharp left (don't actually pass through the squeeze gate - this would take you back up Bishopston Valley crossed earlier) and climb fairly steeply up a stony track. Follow the track until it starts to level out at Pennard Farm. With the farmhouse in front of you turn half left through a gate and then half right, following a painted arrow. Pass directly through a narrow field into a second, larger, field. Cross this field in a straight line, but inclining slightly to your left, to leave it by a stile. Cross the stile and follow the path on the far side as it turns left, keeping a wire fence on your right. Keep an eye open on your left for a small rocky outcrop which offers excellent retrospective views over Pwlldu Bay. Continue along the path past this viewpoint, starting to incline downhill, to emerge on a grassy shelf or plateau. Pick up a path off to the right (slightly obscured by bracken during the summer) leading along the cliff slope and gradually up to the promontory of Pwlldu Head.

From Pwlldu Head a number of paths can be seen, all leading west. You can take any one of them, but if you are in any doubt follow the stone wall on your right, between the field and the headland. Preferably follow the line of the headland to enjoy superb views of the coast right round to the sandy beach at Oxwich. All paths will eventually lead you to Hunts Farm. On arriving at the lane in front of the farm, turn left and follow it back to Southgate and the car park. As an alternative to walking on tarmac it is easier on the feet to keep to a grassy belt running to the left of the lane.

Points of Interest:

1. Bishopston Valley runs from near the church of St Teilo in Bishopston right down to the sea at Pwlldu Bay. It is a green wooded haven, harbouring Bishopston Stream, or Pill. About halfway down the valley is the aptly named Guthole, or Guzzlehole, where the stream can be heard as it runs underground. Although the walk only touches a fairly small section of the valley it is a good representation of the rest. If the opportunity arises the valley stands up admirably as a 'there and back' walk in its own right, especially in spring or early summer when the valley floor is carpeted with bluebells and wild garlic. It can also form part of a circular walk from the church, encompassing Pwlldu Bay, and returning through Bishopston.

2. Just the name Brandy Cove conjures up images of those wonderful lines from Kipling:

'Brandy for the parson, backy for the clerk'
These images are probably well founded, too, as it is very likely named either by or after local smugglers as they plied their illegal trade in the 18th century. The cove was previously known as Hareslade Bay - I prefer Brandy Cove myself.

3. Pwlldu (or Black Pool) Bay sits at the outflow of Bishopston Stream, at the foot of the Bishopston Valley. The name is derived from the presence of a pool formed by the enormous bank of limestone pebbles, or cobbles, at the head of the beach, which 'chink' like fine china when you walk over them. Like other streams in Gower the Bishopston Pill lacks the force to break through this storm bank, except on occasions when the river runs high after heavy rain. In May and June the coastline between Brandy Cove and Pwlldu Bay is alive with the sight and smell of gorse, and you have to fight your way through head-high bracken in stretches to stay afloat. The three houses down on the beach behind the pebble bank were once public houses. One of these was the Beaufort Inn, frequented by quarry workers, when quarrying limestone for lime was a major industry here. The story goes that the landlord never had to pay a penny for any of the wines or brandies he sold to his thirsty customers. It takes little imagination to work out why not!

4. Between Pwlldu Bay and Pwlldu Head is a spot known as Gravesend. It was here, in 1760, that the 'Caesar', a merchant vessel commandeered by the Royal Navy, hit rocks and broke up, with a loss of 68 souls, although local stories tell of 97 dead. Many of those who perished had just been press ganged in Bristol, and were being transported to Plymouth, possibly even shackled below decks. They were buried in a mass grave, below, and just to the east of, Pwlldu Head.

5. In the cliffs between Pwlldu Head and Southgate are two bone caves, Minchin Hole (marked on the OS Landranger Map 159 as Mitchin Hole) and Bacon Hole. Both have revealed animal bones such as hyena, bison and rhinoceros, Minchin Hole yielding up a variety of sea shells too. If you decide to explore these caves further do take care, and don't remove any objects you may find. Access, whilst not impossible, is not particularly easy either. This spectacular stretch of coastline is owned by the National Trust.

Up on the Downs

Llangenydd Moors

To Burry Green

Pub

LLANGENYDD ②

× Hillend Camp Site

← gate

← Steep!

Dunes

• Summit
Rhossili ③
Down

Rhossili Beach

⊖ Hardings Down ①

West Cathan □ East Cathan

Fields ∧

Stream

The Old ④ Rectory □

• Summit

⊖

□ Kingshall

Track

Fernhill Farm □

Wall

○

□ Reservoir

To Middleton

START/FINISH ⇨ CAR PARK

RHOSSILI ⑤

78

Up on the Downs
(Rhossili - Llangenydd - Rhossili)

Access:	The walk starts and ends in the village of Rhossili. Leave Swansea through Bishopston, pass through Kittle, and take the road to Parkmill. Continue through Parkmill to Scurlage. Turn right at Scurlage and follow the road to Rhossili.
Start/Parking:	Car park in Rhossili. At the time of writing the 'all day' charge is £1.50, from March to the end of October. Grid ref. 415880
Distance/Grade:	About 5½ miles (8.8km). Strenuous; mainly because of the long haul up onto Rhossili Down.
Terrain:	The walk covers farm tracks, moorland paths and country lanes. There is a real hill walk feel along the top of Rhossili Down.
Facilities:	The Worms Head Hotel is just across a lane from the car park, and there are loos and a shop nearby. Ideally, time your walk to arrive at the Kings Head, in Llangenydd, in time for lunch.

The Walk:

Leave the car park by the way you came in and follow the road to the sharp right hand bend just past the church. Continue ahead onto a track, and pass through a squeezer gate. Incline right, ascend the hillside of Rhossili Down for a short distance and then make for a stone wall on your right.

Where the stone wall turns sharp right, and a green path continues ahead up to the Down, turn right, alongside the wall. Continue ahead, contouring the hillside rising up on your left and keeping the wall on your right, as far as a white house, again on your right. When level with the house aim ahead and slightly left to meet up with a Welsh Water reservoir. Keeping the reservoir on your right, join a track leading from it to the right as far as a lane.

Turn left in the lane which soon becomes a cinder track and continues ahead in the direction of Hardings Down. Not long after the track turns sharp right, cross over a stile alongside a gate and continue along the track as far as Kingshall. Just before the buildings turn left along a footpath. Keep to the edge of the field, keeping the fence on your left. Make for the stile ahead, crossing a small bridge over a stream to reach it. Crossing into the next field keep the hedge on your left and continue ahead. Cross a further stile and make for the ruined farm buildings ahead. Do not aim for the house standing alone, but, rather, keep ahead to enter the ruins of a long deserted farmyard. Look for a stile behind the farmhouse, and cross it to meet a track at right angles.

Turn left along the track contouring Hardings Down, as far as Cooks Well Farm, down on your left, and look carefully for a path slanting off to the left just after the farmhouse. (Note that whilst there **are** paths up over the Down these are not definitive rights of way). As a guide, the path is almost midway between two telegraph poles on the right hand side of the track and level with the farmhouse. Pass through a gate and, 15 yards (14 metres) later, turn left over a stile, into rough pasture. Pass over another stile into a field. Follow the edge of the field, continuing ahead, and keeping the fence to your right. Cross the stile on the far side of the field and keep to the right. Pass through a gate on your right and turn left along a vague muddy path. Cross over the stile on your left, partly buried in vegetation, and make a bee-line for the tower of Llangenydd church, ahead. At the end of the field, don't take the track on the left, but, instead, cross over a stile and continue ahead to exit the field over a stone stile. This brings you out into the village of Llangenydd, and, as luck would have it, right opposite the King's Head!

With the church on your left continue ahead down the lane, passing both the village well and Well Cottage on your left. Don't take the lane that turns left and carries on down past the church. At the mini-roundabout turn left, downhill. Continue down the lane until you reach Hillend Camping and Caravan Park. Turn left at the grey reception building to pass through a small gate, next to a large gate bearing the National Trust logo, and the name 'Rhossili Down'.

Follow the path half left as it makes its way to the top of the Down, steeply at first, and then more gently as the top is approached. Stay with the path as it firstly passes through the ruins of an old wartime radar station, and then makes its way to the trig point on the further of the two summits. From the trig point, take the path to the right and follow it down to the village of Rhossili below. On your way back to the car park the church of St Mary is well worth a visit. As you pass through the gate at the far end of the churchyard, look out on your left for the Sailors' Corner. (see Points of Interest).

Points of Interest:

1. Hardings Down is one of three hills in the area of Devonian, or old red sandstone, sitting on a bed of carboniferous limestone, the other two being Llanmadoc Hill and Rhossili Down. It rises to a height of just over 500 feet, and is entirely circled by a track at its base. The Down is rich in archaeological history, containing the remains of three iron age earthworks. Views to the east are good, but are blocked off somewhat to the north and west by the higher surrounding heights.

2. The village of Llangenydd has, on a number of occasions, been recorded as the liveliest village in Gower, with all its activities associated with smuggling, festival celebrations and general joie de vivre! It huddles under the three Downs mentioned above in a sheltered hollow within easy walking distance of two sandy beaches. The village church, the largest in Gower, is dedicated to the celebrated Gower saint, Cenydd, the present structure dating from the early 12th century.

3. Rhossili Down, owned by the National Trust, is the highest point on the peninsula, at a little over 600 ft above sea level. The views from the top of the Down are truly dramatic, (subject, of course, to the vagaries of our weather) and especially so from the trig point at the

eastern end, from where the view sweeps majestically from Rhossili along the headland and right out to the Worm itself. Back inland the whole of Gower lies at your feet. The Down contains the remains of two megalithic tombs, known variously as Sweyn's Howes, Sweyn's Houses or the Swine Houses. It is popularly believed that one of these tombs is the resting ground if one Sweyn, a Viking sea lord, after whom it has been suggested Swansea (Sweyn's Eye) has been named.

4. The solitary house half way along the bottom of the Down is the Old Rectory, now owned by the National Trust and rented out as holiday accommodation.

5. Rhossili (or Rhosili, Rhossilly, Rose-hilly, and any number of variations) is a sort of 'second generation' village, the original being buried under the warren at the bottom of the path down to Rhossili beach. Following, allegedly, a spate of very severe storms at the beginning of the 14th century, the old village became engulfed in sand. Remains of an old church and some houses have recently come to light. Some believe the arch to the present doorway of St Mary's church in the village to have been taken from the old church before it finally succumbed to the sand. The 'new' church, dating from the 14th century, was built by the settling Anglo-Normans, and dedicated to St Mary the Virgin. The church contains a memorial to Petty Officer Edgar Evans, born at nearby Middleton, who accompanied Captain Scott on his ill fated expedition to the South Pole in 1912. Look out on your way out of the churchyard (car park end) for the Sailors' Corner, marked by a simple caption engraved on slate. In 1830 a ship fell victim to a violent storm in Fall Bay, just to the east of Tears Point. The unknown victims were buried in this corner of the churchyard. In subsequent years this spot also became the resting ground of any other sailors found under such circumstances.

Have you also noticed that there are no trees here? Research for the book revealed that they cannot survive the harsh batterings meted out by the wind which howls along the peninsula. Apparently, one old ash tree grew in Rhossili some years ago but it did so in a very horizontal manner!

A Coastline Crusade

(Port Eynon - Foxhole Slade - Port Eynon)

Access: The walk starts and ends in the village of Port Eynon. Leave Swansea through Bishopston, pass through Kittle and take the road through Parkmill. Continue along the main South Gower road, passing through Knelston and Scurlage, towards Port Eynon.

Start/Parking: Pay and Display car park at Port Eynon sea front. The all day charge is £2.30 from April 1st to September 30th. Grid ref. 467852

Distance/Grade: 5½ miles (8.8 km). Strenuous; more on account of the constant ascents and descents of the coastline than the length of the walk. Stunning coastal scenery rises above you from every turn so take your camera.

Terrain: Mostly coastal footpaths on the outward leg with fields and tracks on the return journey. The cliff path is loose in places so take care.

Facilities: There are a few shops and cafes near the car park as well as a pub (the Ship Inn) in the village. However, Port Eynon, facilities wise, goes into a state of hibernation in winter. There are loos by the car park, and they, at least stay open all year.

The Walk:

From the car park take the sandy track leading west towards Port Eynon Point. Pass through a gate, and cross a field (a camp site in summer). Pass through another gate to cross a path at right angles. Pass through a third gate (look for a green waymark arrow) into a

A Coastline Crusade

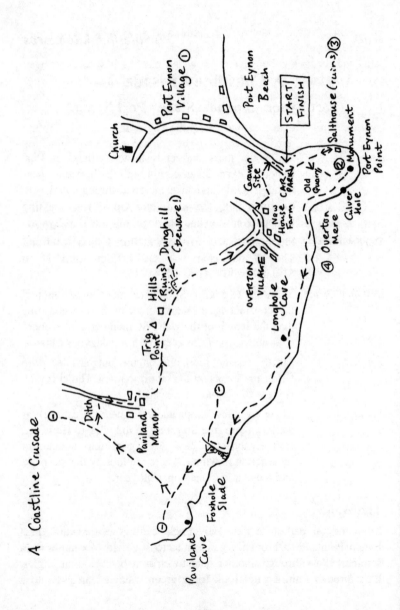

field.

Continue as far as the ruins of Salthouse on your left. From here return to the gate bearing the green waymark arrow and turn left up the path, with hedges either side. Follow the path as it weaves its way through old quarry workings to the top of the headland. Pass, on your left, a prominent memorial stone, erected by The Gower Society. Keeping the cliff edge on your left continue ahead to descend to Overton Mere. The descent path is a little vague here but keeps to the left of the scree remains of old quarries on the headland. From the bottom the path becomes clear again as it circuits the Mere. (From the bottom of the descent, it is possible to turn left back along the rocks to discover the Culver Hole before continuing to Overton Mere).

Cross a stile (with a Glamorgan Wildlife Trust - Overton Mere sign) to the grassland behind Overton Mere. Follow the path around the beach and continue westwards. Where the path splits take the left turn. Cross a stile, about 150 yards (135 metres) this time marked Glamorgan Wildlife Trust - Overton Cliff. Continue ahead crossing a further stile, this time marking Long Hole Cliff. Look up to your right just past here to find Long Hole cave in the cliff above.

Continue ahead to make for a col between two limestone cliffs, the base of the ascent identified by what looks like a number of limekilns turfed over. Descend the other side and continue ahead, crossing a rough stile built into a wall. Again ascend to a col, followed by a descent.

At the bay below this last ascent, turn right and ascend gently, leaving the sea behind you. (Do not continue beyond this point. It involves a rather hairy cliff traverse and is not recommended.) The path follows the line of an old post and wire fence for about 300 yards (270 metres). At the top turn left along the clifftop path.

Continue ahead to cross a stile by the side of a gate (unless the gate is open, which it usually seems to be!). Where the path splits after the stile take the right fork and continue on as far as Foxhole Slade. This is a very deep and obvious gully to the sea, the cliff to the right of the gully exit is where Paviland Cave may be found. Follow the path as it descends into the neck of the gully and turn right over a wooden stile at the lowest point. Do not continue over an iron stile along the cliff path.

Enter a field and continue ahead, keeping the hedge line on your left. Cross two more stiles and then a third, which clips the edge of the field. Continue ahead along the field edge, passing a waymarked path off to your left. Just before a wooden bridge crossing a dyke, turn right along the dyke bank, waymarked on a post. Continue ahead to cross over a stile into a tarmac lane. Turn right along the lane towards Paviland Manor. On reaching the barns, turn left between them, the route marked by a footpath sign. After passing the barns turn right along a waymarked track into a field. Keeping the fence on your right keep ahead to the gateway into the next field. Do not pass through the gateway, but turn left immediately before it along the edge of the field. Keep the hedge, and then the fence, on your right. Exit the field over a stile and make for a stile ahead and slightly to the right. Cross over into another field and look out for a trig point on your left. Also on your left enjoy the panorama of the whole length of the Cefn Bryn Ridge from here. Make for, and slightly to the right of, the remains of Hills Farm.

At the farm ruins cross a stile on your right and turn immediately left. Cross another stile into a field and cross the field, aiming half right to meet the corner of the hedge on your right. (circumvent the monstrous dunghill which sometimes lurks here; it's horrible in the summer!). At the corner turn right, following a waymark sign, and follow the hedge down to a stile at the bottom of the field.

Cross the stile into a scrubby area and follow the path left to join a green lane. Turn right along the green lane and follow it unerringly to Overton. En route it becomes tarmaced. At the village green turn left along the road leading to Port Eynon. Continue ahead for a few hundred yards (a few hundred metres!) as far as New House Farm on your right. About 20 yards (18 metres) past the farm turn right over a waymarked stile. Cross the field to another stile ahead. Cross the stile and continue through the next field to leave it over a stile. Enter the caravan site and turn right onto the track in front.

Follow the track through and then out of the site to emerge in Port Eynon, opposite the Smuggler's Haunt restaurant. From here turn right and return to the start.

Points of Interest:

1. Port Eynon is a small, sleepy, seaside village that comes alive in the summer, and turns over and goes back to sleep in winter. The village takes its name from Eynon, or Einion, an 11th century Welsh prince. It is said that he built a stronghold here, but if he did, nothing remains. The pretty church is dedicated to St Cattwg and houses a very poignant memorial in the corner of the churchyard near the road. It was built in memory of members of the Port Eynon lifeboat crew, who were drowned as part of a brave rescue attempt involving the Glasgow steamer, Dunvegan, in January, 1916. As a result of this tragedy, the lifeboat service was withdrawn from here.

2. Port Eynon Point offers an excellent view of both Port Eynon Bay and the sweep of cliffs off towards the Worms Head. The Point is crowned with a memorial stone, erected by the Gower Society in memory of Gwent Jones and Stephen Lee, possibly prominent members of the Society? It is a very fitting spot for a memorial in any event.

3. All that remains of Salthouse is the gable end and some walls. This was once a pair of cottages that marked the spot where, it is said, John Lucas lived in his mansion in the 16th century. Information boards nearby give a detailed account of the area, and show how, at one time, salt was obtained from the sea water. Around the corner, and built back into the rocks, is the Culver Hole. (see introduction). Whether the Culver Hole was simply a pigeon 'columbarium' or really held some of the Lucas family's dark smuggling secrets we may never know, but it certainly looks dark and full of foreboding. There is a lot of history around these parts!

4. Overton Mere is looked after by the Glamorgan Wildlife Trust, the fields behind the bay being a raised beach, similar to that found between Horton and Oxwich. It became a very popular spot in 1865, when the schooner 'Francis and Ann' came ashore during a gale, and deposited its cargo of oranges all over the beach. As ever, the locals from Overton and Port Eynon were quick on the scene. I'll bet the marmalade had a salty tang for some time afterwards.

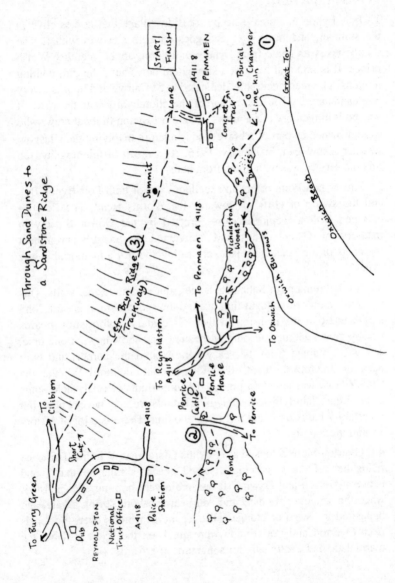

Through Sand Dunes to a Sandstone Ridge

START/FINISH

PENMAEN
A4118

To Burial Chamber
Concrete track
Lime kiln

Great Tor

Oxwich Beach

Lane

Summit

Cefn Bryn Ridge ③ (Trackway)

To Cilibion

Short Cut

To Reynoldston A4118

To Penmaen A4118

Nicholaston Woods

Dunes

To Oxwich

Oxwich Burrows

REYNOLDSTON

National Trust Office

Pub

A4118

Police Station

A4118

Penrice

Castle

Penrice House

To Penrice

② pond

To Bury Green

88

Through Sand Dunes to a Sandstone Ridge
(Penmaen - Reynoldston - Penmaen)

Access: The walk starts and ends in the village of Penmaen. Leave Swansea through Bishopston, pass through Kittle, and take the road to Parkmill. Continue through Parkmill and take a right turn in Penmaen village, opposite Rose Cottage, by a telephone kiosk and bus shelter. Note: do not confuse this with the turn by Penmaen Church, which is passed before you reach the start.

Start/Parking: National Trust car parking area at the eastern end of Cefn Bryn, behind telephone kiosk and bus shelter in Penmaen, opposite Rose Cottage. There is a National Trust honesty box, all donations going towards the upkeep of Trust lands on Gower. Grid ref. 527885

Distance/Grade: About 7 miles (11.3 km). Strenuous; mainly because of the long haul up onto Cefn Bryn

Terrain: The walk covers a clifftop path, woodland tracks, some sand dunes, moorland track and country lanes. The track along the Cefn Bryn ridge is a bit exposed in strong winds.

Facilities: There is a small kiosk near the start, selling ice creams, etc., during the summer months. There is also the King Arthur Hotel, at Reynoldston. The food here comes well recommended so plan the timing of your walk with due consideration for lunchtime!

The Walk:

From the car parking area return to the main road and turn right. Walk as far as the car park/pull in across the road on your left, in front of a row of houses. Turn sharp left through a metal gate, signposted 'Tor Bay 0.8 Km'. Continue down an old farm lane passing some farm buildings on your right. The track gradually narrows to a concrete path, to emerge on Penmaen Burrows.

Take the sandy path on the right which leads to Tor Bay. Do not continue down to the beach, but keep to the right to pass behind a disused lime kiln. Follow the path along the clifftop to a fence and stile. There is a fine view from the stile, both retrospectively to the Great Tor, after which Tor Bay below gets its name, and across the wide sweep of Oxwich Bay. After the stile the path swings a little to the right and then downhill to the dunes below, passing some small limestone outcrops on the way. Take care here as the path drops quite steeply. Continue ahead, crossing two wooden walkways at right angles. These are part of the path coming down to the beach from the village of Nicholaston.

After crossing the second walkway aim for the left hand edge of Nicholaston Woods, ahead. Several paths criss-cross the dunes here so choose your own best line. Pick up a path which follows the seaward side of the woods on your right, and the dunes on your left. This is a good spot to look out for evening primroses, tall stems topped with yellow flowers. Keep an eye open, too, for Butcher's Broom, a small dark green shrub which flowers from January to April and bears bright red berries during the winter. It is said that the shrub earned its name because bunches of it were used by butchers to wipe off their blocks. After a short while, and where the dunes open up to marshland, look for a path leading off right into the woods. This is easy to locate; keep your eyes open for a notice informing you that you are entering a nature reserve. Keep with the path through the woods. Each time it splits take the left fork. Continue ahead until you meet the road leading down to Oxwich from the main South Gower road, just above a small cottage.

Turn right up the hill to the road junction by The Towers, the folly entrance to Penrice House. Turn left along the main road (signposted to Port Eynon) and continue for about 200 yards (182 metres). Cross a stone stile on your left, by a gateway, and clearly marked with a public footpath sign. On entering the field keep ahead and slightly right as far as a line of trees. By some stables turn further right to descend a path, marked with a yellow arrow, to meet the drive to Penrice House, coming in from the right. Turn left along the drive, passing on your left some outbuildings belonging to Penrice House and on your right the ruins of Penrice Castle.

Continue ahead, passing Penrice House on your left, as far as a set of large wrought iron gates. About 10 yards (9 metres) to the left of the gates you will find a stone stile. Cross this into a lane, and make for an aluminium swing gate on the opposite side of the lane entering Millwood, owned by the Forestry Commission, and sometimes referred to as Abertawe Wood.

Pass through the gate into the woods, and follow the green painted arrows. Down on your left are the remains of an old trout pool, possibly constructed to supply the local villagers (with old trout?). Continue ahead as far as a large pond in a clearing on your left. Take the track on the right, leading gently uphill, to leave the woods via a squeezer stile. Continue along the track as far as the main South Gower road once again. Cross the road, and take the lane ahead that leads up to the village of Reynoldston. Either continue along the road as far as Reynoldston and take the right fork up to the Cefn Bryn ridge, or where the lane swings round to the left before Reynoldston, leave it and continue ahead, across open land, straight up the hillside. Either way, you are aiming for the top of the ridge. The benefit of travelling via the village is that it takes you very near the King Arthur Hotel, should you be craving refreshment.

Once you have arrived on the crest of the ridge turn right along a broad and obvious moorland track. This is known by locals as 'Talbot's Way' (or sometimes 'Talbot's Road') named after a former occupant of Penrice House, Mr Christopher Rice Mansel Talbot who used to bring his guests up here to enjoy the views. Continue along the track for the entire length of the ridge. At the eastern end the track descends to meet a narrow lane, but there is a path downhill and off to the right, which is a good corner-cutter if your legs are jaded. Either way, once on the lane, turn right and continue gently downhill to the start.

Points of Interest:

1. It is said that a mediaeval village is buried under the sand at Penmaen Head. Remains of a church were discovered in the last century, and other odd artefacts have been claimed as being found. The rather romantic sounding name attributed to this lost village is Steadwarlango. What is not in doubt is the presence, here, of Pen y Crug, an ancient cromlech, said to be around 4000 to 5000 years old.

2. Penrice Castle is the largest castle in Gower and was built from around 1240 to 1300 by the de Penrice family. With the death of Sir John de Penrice the estate passed to his daughter who married Sir Hugh Mansell, into whose family it then found its way. A large pigeon house was built on to the west wall about 200 years later. When the Mansells moved to Oxwich Castle in the early 15th century Penrice Castle slowly started to fall into disrepair. Penrice House, nearby, was built for Thomas Mansel Talbot in 1775 and is now a private residence. Don't be fooled by the medieval looking gatehouse passed on the junction of the Port Eynon and Oxwich road. As noted earlier it is an elaborate fake, or folly, known locally as The Towers. If you did fall for it you are not alone. Incidentally, the Talbot family of Laycock Abbey, originated here, Fox Talbot being one of the early exponents of photography.

3. The long ridge of Cefn Bryn is made up of old red sandstone and runs west-north west from Penmaen for about 4 miles (6.4 km). Rising to about 600 feet (183 metres) above sea level, the ridge offers superb views across the whole of Gower, and especially of Oxwich Bay. On a clear, crisp autumn day a stride out along Cefn Bryn provides the best boost a jaded spirit could ever need.

Bibliography

A Guide to Gower published by The Gower Society

Rhossili by Robert Lucas. Published by Robert Lucas

Gower Coast Shipwrecks by Carl Smith. Published by Sou'wester Books

The Gower Coast by George Edmunds. Published by Regional Publications (Bristol) Ltd

Portrait of Gower by Wynford Vaughan Thomas. Published by Hale.

The Natural History of Gower by Mary E. Gillham. Published by D Brown & Sons Ltd.

The Story of Gower by Wendy Hughes. Published by Gwasg Carreg Gwalch.